AF394229

Great Women of London

Great Women of London

A History of The Rebels who inspired Others

Esther Freeman

First published in Great Britain in 2025 by
Pen & Sword History
An imprint of Pen & Sword Books Limited
Yorkshire – Philadelphia

Copyright © Esther Freeman 2025

ISBN 978 1 03612 621 6

The right of Esther Freeman to be identified as
Author of this Work has been asserted by her in accordance
with the Copyright, Designs and Patents Act 1988.

A CIP catalogue record for this book is
available from the British Library.

Typeset by Mac Style
Printed in the UK by CPI Group (UK) Ltd, Croydon, CR0 4YY.

The Publisher's authorised representative in the EU for product
safety is Authorised Rep Compliance Ltd., Ground Floor,
71 Lower Baggot Street, Dublin D02 P593, Ireland.
www.arccompliance.com

For a complete list of Pen & Sword titles please contact

PEN & SWORD BOOKS LIMITED
47 Church Street, Barnsley, South Yorkshire, S70 2AS, England
E-mail: enquiries@pen-and-sword.co.uk
Website: www.pen-and-sword.co.uk
or
PEN AND SWORD BOOKS
1950 Lawrence Road, Havertown, PA 19083, USA
E-mail: uspen-and-sword@casematepublishers.com
Website: www.penandswordbooks.com

Contents

Introduction

On a hot July morning, I rose with the dawn chorus, and jumped into a van heading to London Bridge. There, five women climbers solemnly adjusted their climbing gear at the foot of The Shard, Western Europe's tallest building. It is standard practice for a Greenpeace action to provide contact details in event of arrest. This time instructions were left 'in event of death'.

The Greenpeace women took the enormous risk of climbing the Shard because of the threat they believed Shell posed to the Arctic with their reckless oil drilling. These young people felt the multi-national giant was putting the planet at risk, and along with it their futures. From the top of the Shard they unfurled a banner demanding Shell get out of the Arctic. The sacrifice of personal safety felt worth it to halt the existential crisis of climate change.

I had two feet firmly on the ground that day, operating as support crew. It gave me the opportunity to listen to commuters passing by. First there was surprise that people were climbing the Shard; then astonishment that it was women. After the event, I spoke to one of the climbers – Victoria Henry – who explained that gender was an important part of the action. She felt Greenpeace was too often 'beardy boys in boats'.[1] She wanted to present an alternative image, because climate change was everyone's struggle. For some time after her climb, women approached her asking how to get involved in the movement.

This event planted a seed in my mind. It would become an idea that turned into a five-year research project, exploring how far women would go for the causes they believe in.

It wasn't always easy to find stories of heroic women. I scanned copies of the iconic feminist publication, Spare Rib; dug through endless boxes in the archives at the Bishopsgate Institute; and The Women's Library's rich collection of oral history interviews. With the help of a brilliant and dedicated team of volunteers, I collected new oral history interviews, so the stories of today's hidden heroes would be remembered.

The archive of materials I collected (now happily housed at The Bishopsgate Institute) challenged many of the beliefs I held about feminism. Stories I thought I knew sometimes turned out to be wrong, or at least skewed towards a particular retelling of events, usually from the perspective of the rich, white women. I was forced to unpick my perceptions of race, and why many women don't comfortably associate with the term feminist. Most of all, I was left considering: why are so few of these stories in traditional history books, or taught in schools?

According to Art UK, only 4% of statues in the capital are of women. In fact, there are more statues of animals than women. Enthusiasts on X/Twitter alleged there are more statues of goats than women of colour. This claim is a little woolly, but the fact it was easily believed says a lot about the state of women's heritage.

Since second wave feminism, people have been retrieving women from the 'dustbin of history'. Leon Trotsky is credited with the origins of this phrase, but it was coopted by the British feminist cartoonist, Jacky Fleming, to describe the battle to get women's stories heard. In recent years, female historians have been shoving their male counterparts along the book shelves, forcing space for women's stories. Yet like the few statues that exist, these books tend to focus on the wealthy, elite, and predominantly white individuals. We are not short of statues, or books, about Queen Victoria or Emmeline Pankhurst. It's harder to find any of Olive Morris, leader of the Brixton Black Women's group, housing rights campaigner, and member of the British Black Panthers. Following the death of George Floyd, and the toppling of the Edward Colston statue in Bristol in June 2020, campaigners launched a petition to erect a statue of Olive in Windrush Square in Brixton. At the time of writing, there is still no such statue.

Great Women of London aims to tell the stories you haven't heard before. The stories of mostly working class women, who despite their limited economic and social means, still inspired great change; changes to society that many of us benefit from today. Most of these women worked through unions, cooperatives and tenants associations, knowing the oppressed can be most powerful when they act together. Where possible, I've tried to name individual women. This is not only to celebrate their specific achievements, but to prevent others stepping in and claiming credit. This is evident in the story of the match women of Bow, whose famous strike of 1888 many believe was led by Annie Besant, the socialist and women's rights activist. While notable in her many great deeds, Besant in fact opposed the women striking, as historian Louise Raw robustly argues in her book Striking A Light. Besant believed they'd simply be replaced by other young women, desperate for work. She encouraged a boycott instead. The match women stuck to their guns, and were proved right. Their tenacity and bravery in the face of such perceived odds should be remembered. To do that, it helps if we know at least some of their names.

This book will challenge the idea that first wave feminism was simply about gaining the vote. In East London, it was highly contested whether the campaign for the vote would change anything. Many leading socialist thinkers, such May Morris and Rose Witkop, thought it a distraction. Witkop said: 'How shall we benefit if instead of electing our masters – as we do today – we elect his wife to govern us.'[2]

Even Sylvia Pankhurst, who split from the Women's Socialist and Political Union (WSPU) run by her mother and sister, knew they had to fight for more than inclusion in the franchise. For them, the suffrage struggle was a fight against poverty, sexual exploitation and housing issues.

Many argue that the women's movement died after 1918, when the vote was finally granted. The evidence does not support this theory. While it's true that without the issue of the vote to hold them together, great chasms emerged in the women's movement. Beyond the desire for the vote, they often held vastly different views on everything from prostitution to pacifism. Yet the fight for equality did continue for many throughout the first half of the twentieth century. There was the little matter of the vote only being granted to women who met the property qualification, excluding most poorer women in East London. Many working class women continued to lobby parliament until 1928, when full suffrage equality was finally achieved. During the 1930s, women took a leading role in the fight for housing rights, due to their unique position in the home. Although missing from many retellings, they were at the forefront of the fight against fascism, including during the Battle of Cable Street.

During WW2, most women were tied up in a basic struggle for survival to actively campaign, and too exhausted post war. It would largely fall to their daughters in the 70s and 80s to take up the mantle. Yet when these women came of age, London had changed considerably. In East London, Bengalis replaced Jews on the streets of Shoreditch. While some of the issues remained the same – housing, labour rights, equal pay – the rise of the National Front led this new community to fight for spaces safe from the threat of violence.

This so-called second wave feminism didn't always reflect the new demographics of the capital. In 1970, Miss World activists were criticised for not including the views of women of colour. For Jennifer Holsten from Grenada – crowned the first black Miss World – the competition was a huge step forward for her community. Since the 1950s, radicals like Claudia Jones, founder of the Notting Hill Carnival, had been using beauty pageants to fight racism, promoting notions of black beauty and black pride.

Yet it was the civil rights movement in the US that inspired the women's movement. Also with their backs up against the wall, the queer community followed their lead too. Most notably this included the Stonewall Riots in New York in 1969, which led to the formation of the gay Pride march and the Gay Liberation Front (GLF). While women were in the minority in the movement, their impact was significant. Yet within a few years, queer women would find themselves politically homeless, feeling sidelined within groups like GLF London; while being told their issues were personal matters by the Women's Liberation Movement leaders.

East London is a vastly different place from 150 years ago, with the anarchist social clubs replaced by glass and steel of multi-national companies. Yet the capital itself remains a hotbed of activism. Issues have shifted, with the fight against climate change replacing the threat of nuclear war. The nature in which women campaign has also changed. The spirit of collective activism was crushed along with the miners in the 1980s. Many young activists today develop their politics around individual identities, and so-called wokeness. And of course, social media replaces printed pamphlets, and speeches from the top of wheelbarrows. Yet clicktivism is often seen as too passive for meaningful change. And although this individualistic approach to social justice started from legitimate grievances, it's increasingly criticised for creating a blame-based culture.

Told in four parts, Great Women of London explores each of these generations through the stories of individual women, and the collectives they belonged to. In researching these stories, I admit, at times I've developed para-social relationships. This is often due the close proximity of their stories with my own. Like Milly Witkop in chapter two, my great-grandparents fled the Russian Empire, finding subsistence through tailoring in the East End. The links I could see with my own life helped the individuals come alive, and showed me whose shoulders I stand on. Therefore, I chose to use their first names in telling their stories, so that others can feel the same connection. These were real women, whose actions have shaped our lives in extraordinary ways.

I wonder what these class-conscious, unionised women of the past, who'd march from Bow to Westminster, think of the way we campaign today? Would they be angry that things they fought so hard for, are now taken for granted? As the repeal of Roe vs Wade in the US shows, women's rights can be lost as well as won. Some foolishly think Britain wouldn't be so reactionary, but this ignores the march to the right of politics across Europe. We must learn the lessons of our sisters of the past, and protect what they fought so hard for. The way to start is by discovering their stories.

Part I

1880–1918

Chapter 1

Match Women Rise Up!

When Samuel Webster saw the women coming down Bow Road, they were singing. They weren't singing their usual tunes from the music halls; these songs were marching and militant.

It was one of the coldest Julys most could remember, with thunderstorms and even snow. The streets were muddy, which was thrown up by the hooves of horses. It mixed with soot from the chimneys, making the air thick and hard to breathe. Samuel loitered by the side of the road, watching as the numbers of marchers swelled. He recognised the women from the match factory: they were young, some not much more than 12; they took pride in their appearance, using the few spare pennies they had for colourful feathers for their hats; yet their clothes looked worn and in need of repair. There were others with them – men and women – wearing finer outfits, and carrying political banners.

People in the offices overhead leaned out of the windows. A shower of pennies rained down, and the women stopped singing as they scrambled to pick them up. The ground swept clean of coppers, they waved at their donors before taking up singing again.[1]

It was summer of 1888, and the East End was burning with agitation. A few days earlier, those known as the match girls had walked out of the Bryant & May factory. Although some may have been very young[2], and indeed, called themselves 'girls', in this retelling of the story I will call them women. This is to distance them from the Hans Christian Anderson story, The Little Match Girl. These women were far from waifs. They had a reputation for being rough and rowdy, settling differences with their fists in the streets. And their determination in taking on one of the largest companies in Victorian Britain was not the action of little girls.

It would be nice not to force this point through language, but both the media at the time, which was overwhelmingly hostile, and treatment by historians who downplay their importance, prove it necessary. The facts are clear – these were smart, brave women, who changed the face of trade unionism in Britain.

The match women rose up in an era where Britain ruled the world. Despite the country's prosperity, much of the wealth remained in the hands of a privileged few. The workers who kept the fires of the industrial revolution burning – or indeed made the matches to light those fires – saw little of the Empire's wealth. What's more, their work could be lethal. And there were few jobs more dangerous than making matches.

William Bryant and Francis May opened their first match factory in Bow, East London in 1843. By 1860, they were selling 27.9 million boxes a year. In 1861, they relocated their growing business to a three-acre site on Fairfield Road. By the 1880s they employed nearly 5000 people, most of them female and Irish, or of Irish descent.[3]

Their success was built on the back of sweated labour – crowded workspaces, with poor ventilation and lighting, and little or no breaks at all. Workers toiled for up to 14 hours a day, six days a week. Wages were low, especially for women. And they rarely took home what was promised, due to a system of fines for offences as trivial as a messy workbench, dropping matches or going to the toilet without permission.

One of the worst things about the factory was working with white phosphorous, which was used in the tips of matches. Breathing in the chemical caused irritation to the mouth and throat, leading to shortness of breath; getting it on your skin caused burns, blisters, and severe pain; prolonged exposure caused kidney, liver and heart damage, as well as the dreaded 'phossy jaw', a type of bone cancer that caused painful abscesses in the mouth, facial disfigurement and fatal brain damage. The dangers had been known for sometime, with Charles Dickens writing about it in 1852. So Bryant & May would've been aware of the risks when they opened the Fairfield Road site. Yet they chose not to move over to the safer red phosphorous, as it was more expensive.

Bryant & May had a policy of concealing rather than preventing cases of phosphorous poisoning. A woman turning up at work with a swollen face was ordered to have all her teeth pulled, or be dismissed. Some took preventative action, hiding symptoms of toothache for fear of dismissal. There wasn't much they could do to protect themselves, as there wasn't anywhere to eat other than the factory floor. Before white phosphorous was banned in the early twentieth century, it's estimated that around 1 in 10 workers developed phossy jaw.[4]

The Fabians meet

On 15th June 1888, leading trade unionist, Clementina Black, spoke at a Fabian Society meeting about the state of female labour in Britain. Henry Hyde Champion claimed that Bryant & May were taking 20% dividends for shareholders, while paying female workers starvation wages. Journalist and activist, Annie Besant decided to investigate the next day. She went to the factory with fellow Fabian, Herbert Burrows. They spoke to workers outside the factory gates, and heard about the long hours, fines and low pay. A week later, Annie published her infamous article, White Slavery In London, in socialist newspaper, The Link.

Bryant & May demanded workers sign a document stating the claims were untrue, but the women refused. The factory owners threatened to sue Annie for libel, but she'd already dodged prison for publishing a book about birth control, and wasn't easily intimidated. So Bryant & May drew up a list of suspected ring leaders.

The troublemakers

Alice Francis was born on 27th June 1862 in Bethnal Green. Her father was a bootmaker, which was a skilled but poorly paid craft. Like many girls of her background, once Alice finished school she moved out of home and into domestic service.

There's no record of what life was like there for her, but domestic service was notorious for being backbreaking drudgery, with long hours for little pay. There were endless rules and regulations, and you were expected to know your place. Punishments for stepping out of line could be harsh. Then there were the master's wandering hands that so many young women endured. There was little point in complaining, because who would believe the maid? Maybe this is why Alice left service. Or maybe like so many others, it was the better pay offered by the newly opened factories. Whatever the reason, Alice found work at the Bryant & May factory, where she became friends with Sarah Chapman. It was a relationship that shaped both their lives.

If you headed down Mile End Road, past the People's Palace, and turned left at The Swan pub, you'd come to a little alleyway leading through to a courtyard. It no longer exists, and there are no surviving photos, but courts like these were considered some of the worst homes in the East End. The housing was dilapidated and sanitary conditions grim, with one standpipe providing water for all the homes in the courtyard. Broken windows were repaired with rags stuffed in gaps, and bannisters were removed for firewood. They were cold, smelt of damp, and had bugs in the walls. According to the industrialist and social reformer, Charles Booth, who conducted extensive surveys of working-class areas in the nineteenth century, Swan Place was 'poor' with most people earning between 18–21 shillings a week. This is where Sarah Chapman lived with her parents, and six brothers and sisters.

Sarah was born on 31st October 1862, and at one point was listed on the census as 'scholar'. This suggests she received some education, and could read and write. Despite this, most working-class women like her had no time for diaries or letters. Even if she had, few archives would consider them important enough to preserve. Such scant evidence poses a challenge when trying to understand the individual lives of the poor. So my understanding of Sarah's life is pieced together from general documentation about the lives of working-class women in Victorian Britain. This includes oral histories from other match women, passed down the generations.[5]

When Sarah returned from the factory she probably helped with chores, before sitting down for a meal of bread and dripping. It's not known if

Sarah's mother made match boxes at home for a few extra pennies, but many families did. Sarah would've helped alongside her younger siblings, often late into the evening. Once glued together, the boxes would be spread across the floor to dry, ready for one of the younger children to take to the factory the next day. Only then would Sarah have a moment to put her feet up, with a quick puff of a pipe before bed.

It's likely she shared a bedroom with some, if not all of her brothers and sisters. She probably shared a bed with them too. Throughout the night, she might suffer wriggling younger siblings; coughing of the ill; and crying babies. Yet she would still rise at the crack of dawn, scramble out of bed, and begin her morning chores, including cleaning out the grate and laying a new fire. She'd grab any pair of shoes she could find in the cupboard under the stairs, before heading out the door to begin another 12–14-hour shift at the factory. She'd done the same, six days a week, since she was at least 19 years old, just like her mother and older sister Mary.

On the 5th July 1888, Sarah arrived at work to find it buzzing. Eliza Martin, Jane Wakeling, Kate Sclater, Mary Driscoll and Sarah's friend Alice were named on the list of troublemakers. All had been sacked. The chatter started as whispers, before voices rose declaring something must be done. 'It just went like tinder,' an un-named match woman said. 'One woman began, and the rest said 'yes' so we all went out.'[6] Around 1400 women, and some men, walked out in solidarity with those who'd been sacked. Among them was Sarah, in support of her friend Alice.

On the 6th July, The Star reported that the 'whole factory is lying idle'. Bryant & May panicked, and offered to reinstate the sacked women. Realising their power, the strikers refused. They were now out for far more.

Not a lot is known about Sarah's politics prior to the strike. She may have attended one of the local Socialist Sunday schools, which were growing in popularity in East London. Or she may have been influenced by her father, who worked down the docks. The Great Dock Strike was still a year away, but the Dock, Wharf, Riverside and General Labourers Union had formed a year before, and chances are he was a member. But the match women were not unionised, so needed help and direction.

They'd written to Annie Besant the day before. Having a better education than some of the others, it's believed Sarah may have been the author of that letter. It read:

My Dear Lady, – we thank you very much for the kind interest you have taken in us poor girls, and hope that you will succeed in your undertakings. Dear lady, you need not trouble yourself about the letter I read in the Link that Mr. Bryant sent you, because you have spoken the truth, and we are very pleased to read it. Dear lady, they are trying to get the poor girls to say that it is all lies that has been printed, and trying to make them sign papers to say it is lies; dear lady, no one knows what we have to put up with, and we will not sign them. We all thank you very much for the kindness you have shown to us. My dear lady, we hope you will not get into any trouble on our behalf, as what you have spoken is quite true; dear lady, we hope that if there will be any meeting we hope you will let us know it in the book. I have no more to say at present, from yours truly, with kind friends wishes for you, dear lady, for the kind love you have shown us poor girls. Dear lady do not mention the date this letter was written or I might have put my or our names, but we are frightened, do keep that as a secret, we know you will do that dear lady.

After the walk out, around 200 women went to Annie's offices in Bouverie Street in the City of London. Annie invited in a deputation of three. Sarah was one of them, lending further evidence to the theory she'd written the original letter. Annie later recalled of the meeting:

Up came three women and told their story: they had been asked to sign a paper certifying that they were all treated well and contented, and that my statements were untrue; they refused. 'You spoke up for us,' explained one, 'and we weren't going back on you.' A girl pitched on as their leader, was threatened with dismissal; she stood firm; next day she was discharged for some trifle, and they all threw down their work, some 1400 of them, and then a crowd started off to me to ask what to do next.[7]

Annie favoured a boycott of Bryant & May matches. She felt a strike wouldn't work, as the women would quickly be replaced by other desperate souls eager for employment. Yet she agreed to help them anyway, and began plans for a committee.

On 8th July, they held the first meeting on Mile End Waste. They agreed to create a strike register, to provide funds for those who'd walked out. The Star & Pall Mall Gazette collected donations from their readers, but the match women collected far more within their own community. The East London Advertiser reported at the time:

During the strike the principal streets and thoroughfares of East London, especially the Mile End Road, have been swarmed with the girls, who were generally accompanied by male members of the lowest orders. The [Mile End] Waste every morning has generally presented a strange spectacle of some 500 or 600 people lolling about doing nothing. Some of the girls march up and down the streets soliciting coppers, and were quite willing to pour their tale of hardship into every sympathetic ear. On Tuesday morning, opposite the Earl Grey [public house], a van load of pink roses were flung into the street by two men who had charge of the carts and it afterward appeared that the roses had been sent down – by whom it did not transpire – to be worn by the strikers as badges.

Friends and family stood by the match women too. Their solidarity was legendary, often arranging collections if someone fell ill, lending clothes, boots or a crust of bread. This time was no exception:

… few people could fail to be touched by the way in which the girls were determined to stand together at all costs. 'I can pawn this for you', 'I'll lend you that', in every direction, girls might be seen plotting how they could help one another on until Bryant and May gave them their pennies.[8]

On 10th July, Annie Besant took 56 of the striking women to the House of Commons. Considering Sarah's leading role so far, chances are she was one of them. A deputation of 12 met with MPs, Robert Cunningham Graham and Charles Conybeare. They shared stories of hardship, and the reasons behind their strike.

On 11th July, the strike register opened. Sarah attended with her sister Mary, and around seven hundred boys, girls, men and women signed up. It would've been more, but many had left the city to go fruit and hops picking, as was the tradition amongst those in the East End during the summer months.

By 12th July, momentum had grown. Toynbee Hall, established to address the causes and impacts of poverty, added their support. Moved by their meeting with the match women, Robert Cunningham Graham and Charles Conybeare raised the matter in parliament.

The situation was an escalating PR disaster for Bryant & May, yet it took a further five days before the directors met with the London Trades Council, and then the strike committee. The meeting was a success, with all demands met and terms agreed in principle. This included the abolition of fines; ending deductions for equipment; a separate room for meals away from their work stations; formation of a union; and all those sacked reinstated.

The significance of this victory can't be overstated. This was one of the biggest and most powerful employers in East London, and a group of poor teenagers defeated them. On 4th August, the inaugural meeting of the Union of Match Makers took place at Stepney Hall, with 468 new unionists enrolling. Sarah Chapman was elected to the union committee, along with her friend Alice Francis. In a photo taken that first day, they stand with their arms linked, a wry smile on Sarah's face.

The success of the strike energised Sarah. She became the first elected TUC (Trades Union Congress) representative from the newly formed match workers union, attending the International TUC Conference in London with Annie Besant. She went again in 1890, when the TUC was in Liverpool. There are sadly no records of her feelings, so we can only imagine her excitement at what was probably her first time outside of

London. Reaching the conference alongside five hundred other delegates must have been exhilarating. But how did she feel being one of only ten women there? This marks her out as a trailblazer within the women's labour movement, even if history doesn't formally record her as such.

At the conference she was more than a passive observer. She stood as a seconder on the Truck Act motion, which opposed deductions to wages for equipment, damaged goods or fines. This was something Sarah knew about all too well, so seconding was a clear act of solidarity. Sarah went beyond concerns of her own trade, making a clear political stand.

Life after Bryant & May

Sarah continued working at the Bryant & May factory after the strike. She remained there until 1891, when she married Charles Dearman, a cabinet maker. They moved to Bethnal Green and Sarah became pregnant. She gave birth to a son, who they named Charles. Tragically, her little boy died at only ten days old. Infant death was common – only one in three children in East London survived beyond the age of five. Diseases like scarlet fever and measles took countless children, while overcrowded and damp conditions put babies at high risk of tuberculosis. Although death was all around them, the idea that they got used to it, as some will suggest, dehumanises working class communities. The death of a child will always be incredibly painful.

Sarah had four more children, but the tragedy didn't end there. In 1921, she lost her daughter, Elizabeth Rose, and her husband the following year. Her son Charles served in both world wars, but died of his injuries in 1945. Of her six children, she was survived by only three.

This may explain why there are no further records of her political work after the high of the 1890 TUC conference. Although she saw the establishment of the East London Federation of Suffragettes (ELFS) in 1914; witnessed the General Strike in 1926; and the Battle of Cable Street in 1936, there are no accounts of her being involved with any of them. That's not to say she wasn't – only that no evidence exists. It's possible she was there, or even quietly supporting from the sidelines.

I find it hard to believe that after such a leading role in the match workers strike, Sarah simply stopped. That's not to say this doesn't happen for women. As we will see in later chapters, burn out from activism is well documented, while others choose to step back once their fight is won. The fact Sarah continued her involvement with the TUC suggests this wasn't the case for her. This lends weight to the theory that demands of family life, and emotional strain, may have led to her dissolving involvement.

Sarah died when she was 83 years old, and was buried in a pauper's grave in Manor Park, which suggests financial hardship followed into her later years. That her surviving children couldn't find the funds to properly mark her passing, only adds to the sadness, especially considering her importance in social history.

In 2017, Sarah's great grand-daughter, Sam Johnson, began a campaign to change that. With the support of Unite London and Eastern Region, and GMB National[9], they funded a headstone to give Sarah the tribute she deserves. However, with burial space in London running out, cemeteries look for ways to reclaim land through re-mounding. This is a process where they remove headstones, the ground is levelled and new earth laid down. This was the destiny for Sarah's grave. Sam appealed to the Ministry of Justice, and they offered to chair a meeting with the people who run the cemetery. However, it's a privately owned business, and they refused the appeal. The remounding has now taken place, with the headstone stored at the TUC headquarters, while they wait for the ground to settle. It will then be placed on the plot. Sam continues to fight for a lasting memorial for Sarah.[10]

Their influence

Leading radicals of the day documented the significance of the match women's strike. William Morris commented:

> ... even people in such a wretched condition as these poor match girls can make themselves felt temporarily, and can help swell the mass of opposition to the manufacturers' ideal, to wit, human machinery

which will give not more, but less trouble than the machinery of mere dead matter.[11]

Despite this grand fanfare by one of Britain's leading socialists, this hasn't stopped contemporary historians diminishing the match women's efforts. In Socialist Liberals and Labour: The Struggle for London 1855–1914, Paul Thompson states that the strike was '… relatively isolated and consequently, given exaggerated publicity.'[12] John Marriott shares this view in his book, Beyond the Tower, claiming their influence is overstated.

Yet in Striking A Light, Louise Raw clearly details the influence they had on the 1889 dock workers strike, which saw 100,000 walk out in what is considered the start of new unionism. In his memoir, dock strike leader, Ben Tillet, described the match women's strike as 'the beginning of the social convulsion.'[13] Annie Besant came to address 5000 dock workers shortly after the match women's strike, and many dockers went to the Union of Match Workers for advice.[14]

There are also community factors. Like Sarah, many match women were fathered by or married to dock workers. They all lived and worked in the same small area, and knew each other intimately. There were close links within socialist circles too. Clementina Black was friends with Eleanor Marx, a leading figure in the Gas Workers and General Labourers Union, who also quickly followed the match women's strike. At all levels, this was an inter-connected group of people, none of whom worked in isolation.

Their legacy

Three months after the strike, Jack the Ripper began his murderous rampage – a series of events that forever stained the area in the public's mind. One day during this gruesome period, a letter arrived at the Bryant & May factory signed by 'John Ripper' threatening to 'pay a visit' to female employees, detailing what would occur in brutal terms, and claiming to be motivated by the strike. No match woman was murdered by the notorious serial killer, and the letter was probably a hoax, yet it illustrates what the women stirred up in the patriarchy.[15]

Despite this hostility, the women's influence was still felt. A few years after the strike, it became a requirement to notify public health officials of the number of cases of phosphorous poisoning. In 1898, the Chief Inspector of Factories reported 21 cases, although it would take a further three years for Bryant & May to agree to stop using it. In 1908, there was an outright ban in Britain, with a two-year grace period. Although we can't claim this is a direct result of the match women's actions, no big legislative changes happen in a single step. The strike at Bryant & May undoubtably drew more public attention to the issue, laying the stepping stones to that important legislation.

Despite their impact and influence, there's no statue to the match women (although a campaign exists to erect one[16]). While writing this book, English Heritage finally installed a blue plaque for the match women at Bow Quarter, site of the former Bryant & May factory.[17] While a huge step forward, the women themselves remain nameless – a mass of females with no individual identities. They did have names though, including Sarah Chapman, Alice Francis, Mary Driscoll, Eliza Martin, Eliza Askew and more. It's time we properly honoured them.

Chapter 2

Milly Rise Up!

There was nothing special about the narrow terrace building on Jubilee Street in Whitechapel, other than the hundreds of people surrounding it trying to get in. It was 3rd February 1906, and the opening night of The Workers' Friend Club, founded by the German anarchist, Rudolph Rocker. Inside, at least 800 people packed the main hall, with smaller rooms to the side stacked with books on socialism, anarchism and communism. Another adjoining room housed the printing offices of Der Arbayter Fraynd (The Workers' Friend), a Yiddish language newspaper that was gaining popularity beyond the Jewish community. On this day, the printers were off as the young radicals crowded into the main hall for the opening of their new political and social home.

The smell of pickled herring, gefilte fish and coffee filled the air, as Rudolph stood on a platform addressing the packed crowds. He read out messages of congratulations from almost every Jewish trade union in the country. He was interrupted by a storm of cheering and clapping – Peter Kropotkin, the Russian revolutionary, had entered the room. People shook his hand and patted him on the back as he squeezed his way to the front. Rudolph was nervous – Peter's doctor had ordered him to refrain from any public gatherings due to his heart. Over the noise of the crowd he begged him to rest. Grumbling under his breath, Peter waved him aside and mounted the platform to the delighted cheers of the audience[1]

Kropotkin would not be the only Russian revolutionary to enter through the doors of the Jubilee Street Club. Lenin used it for one of his first London speeches, and would pop by at other times to drink Russian tea. But these grand men of the revolution can be read about in any number of places. Instead, I want to tell you about another pioneer at that opening night; a woman who'd become one of the most important organisers, speakers and writers of the twentieth century women's movement. Yet she's missing from most history books.

On 3rd March 1877, Milly Witkop came screaming into the world. She was born into a poor Jewish family in Zlatopil in what is now Ukraine. She was followed by three sisters – Polly, Fanny and Rachel (aka Rose). Her father was a patch cutter,[2] and in order to feed their growing family, her mother worked as a trader in the local market. They lived together in a shtetl, the Yiddish word for settlement. They usually consisted of tenement buildings, packed closely together. There were no gardens, as Jews were not permitted to own land. It was a basic life, with a constant fight against poverty, but the community was close. Milly's parents were devout, embracing Yiddishkeit, which literally translates as Jewishness. Helping others was core to their way of living.

At the time, Ukraine was part of the Russian Empire. Tsar Alexander II was relatively tolerant towards Jews. Following his assassination in 1881, society turned. The ascension of Alexander III brought with it a new era of terror. There was police brutality along with discriminatory laws, which suppressed Jewish civil liberties. Jews were wrongly accused of the murder of Alexander II. Anti-Jewish groups unleashed reprisals, claiming the support of the government. Russian media collaborated, with unrestrained anti semitic propaganda.

Some of the earliest attacks on Jews took place in Ukraine, so Milly and her family found themselves in the heart of the troubles. All around them neighbours were packing up their few belongings and fleeing. But you needed money to leave, and Milly's family had little of that. They agreed Milly should go alone, and the others would join her later. Aged only 18, she began her epic journey. She was one of 1.9 million Jews who fled the Russian Empire between 1881 and 1912. Most went to the US, but many arrived in Britain. Of those, 75% made London their home. This is where Milly settled.[3]

A new vision

Alone and with barely any money, like many other Jewish migrants Milly found work in the East End tailoring sweatshops, making mass, cheap clothing or uniforms for the armed forces and prisons. Pay was pitifully low, and the conditions appalling. The workers sewed for over 12 hours per day in unbearably stuffy and cramped rooms. Until the invention of the sewing machine in 1854, it was done by hand, in poor light. Milly probably bought her own candles, and got only six shillings for a dozen shirts.[4]

Milly was deeply religious, but this new environment was so different from her home town in Ukraine. People worked on the Sabbath, and did many things contrary to Jewish principals. Half measures were not in Milly's nature – whatever she did she committed to fully. So she distanced herself from organised religion. Before long, a new world view opened up. She embraced it with the same fervour she had for her faith.

Through a chance meeting with a local trade unionist, she learnt about the causes of her terrible working conditions. New political ideologies took shape and she threw herself into books, reading all she could on these new libertarian ideas. Milly loved learning, possessing a fierce intelligence. She formed strong opinions of her own, which she expressed with eloquence.

With revolutionary spirit rising up all around her, she took part in local strikes and international demonstrations. She joined the Workers' Friend Group and wrote for Der Arbayter Fraynd. Established in 1885, the paper began as a socialist publication, later developing anarchist values. It questioned the legitimacy of authority in society, believing humanity functions best without hierarchy. Der Arbayter Fraynd had a distinctly Jewish feel, embracing the community's cultural traditions and developing the Jewish labour movement. This is probably where Milly met Rudolph Rocker. Although from different backgrounds, they connected through a shared passion for politics. They went on to spend the next six decades together, sharing love, life and a struggle for workers' liberation.

The rest of the family

For three years, Milly denied herself 'every extra penny's worth of food'[5] until she was able to bring her parents and sisters to London. This included Rose, who shared her revolutionary spirit. Rose was particularly interested in women's sexual, political and economic freedom. Yet like many East End women, she wasn't enamoured by Emmeline Pankhurst's suffragette movement. In her view, they were a group of mainly middle and upper class women who held no interest in the emancipation of the working classes. In fact, she didn't believe the vote was relevant to the struggle at all. She accurately predicted that if women were enfranchised, the working classes would be excluded. Even if they did have it, she questioned what difference it would make to their lives.[6]

This positioned her apart from even the ELFS, who believed the vote could bring economic freedoms for working class women. It's not known if Milly held these views. Her and Rose shared many political beliefs, and I've never found reference to Milly's involvement in the ELFS, even though she lived shoulder to shoulder with them. Despite modern depictions of a united women's suffrage movement, many socialist women felt the vote was a distraction. Eleanor Marx and May Morris also called for economic liberation before electoral reform.

Whatever Milly's views on female suffrage, it wasn't a priority. Her focus was on Der Arbayter Fraynd, co-editing the publication with Rudolph. In 1900, they set up another newspaper called *Germinal*, which focused on philosophy and literature, using a libertarian approach to analyse them. It outsold Der Arbayter Fraynd, reaching far beyond London, claiming readers in Paris, Berlin, Cairo, Cape Town, Johannesburg, and across the US. Then three days before Christmas in 1907, Milly's journalistic career was temporarily put on hold as their son Fermin was born.

Family life

The young family lived in a modest home in London's East End. People of all nationalities and races visited, who Milly welcomed with warmth and charm, acting as mother to friends and comrades younger than her. In the evenings, she and Rudolph read aloud to each other from books by writers of every nationality and period. While they didn't have much, and at times suffered hardship, their intense love brought great happiness. You couldn't mention Rudolph without Milly, the pair were so inseparable. Rudolph said of their relationship: 'We found each other, and although each came from an entirely different worlds, we built a world of our own together. This, alone, was the essence of our union.'[7]

In 1912, organising opportunities arose for Milly and Rudolph. The dockers went on strike, bringing the docks to a halt for two months. In an act of international solidarity, Milly arranged for the children of the dock workers to stay in the homes of Jewish comrades. As summer approached, a strike started among West End tailors for better piece rates. On 2nd May, The Times of London reported 7000–8000 workers at one strike meeting.[8] Rudolph had spent years trying to encourage Jewish garment workers in the East End to properly unionise. He seized the opportunity, organising a rally in Whitechapel. Around 8000 workers packed inside a hall, with 3000 more outside on the street. They took a vote, and two days later 13,000 garment workers walked out. They organised joint meetings between the dockers and tailors, building solidarity between the two communities.

War

The uprising was cut short in 1914 when international tension exploded into war. On 4th August, Britain entered the conflict. That same month, Rudolph wrote an essay predicting 'a period of mass murder such as the world has never known before.'[9]

The impact on working class communities went beyond the sacrifices made on the front line. By 1914, around 750,000 men had enlisted. Without workers, many factories closed down. Having lost their main breadwinner, and with no other work, working class families became destitute. What's more, as food was sent overseas to feed the troops, and less arrived back because of German submarine attacks, prices spiralled.

By the end of the war, costs had more than doubled and hunger took hold. Milly and Rudolph set up a soup kitchen to feed the community. In October, Rudolph published a statement in Der Arbayter Fraynd refusing to support the allied cause. He called it a 'contradiction of everything we have fought for'. Soon after the publication of his statement, he was interned at Alexandra Palace as an enemy alien. In 1915, the government closed down Der Arbayter Fraynd. The British anarchist movement never recovered from this blow.

With Rudolph imprisoned, Milly continued the fight alone. This left her in a vulnerable position. As war-based patriotism reached fever pitch, anti semitism once more reared its head. Following the introduction of conscription in January 1916, The East London Observer complained of: 'Jew boys, as they are termed, who hang about street corners and public houses, the cheap foreign restaurants and similar places ought to be made to do something for the country they honour with their presence.'[10] In fact, unnaturalised Jews weren't allowed to join the British Armed Forces, even voluntarily. While many naturalised Jews enlisted, many didn't for good reasons. They hadn't fled violent pogroms in Russian only to fight for its ally.

As the relentless demand for soldiers continued, the Government changed the law, allowing 'friendly aliens' to enlist. The demand came with a threat to deport anyone who refused to Russia. The Jewish community's position was fractured. While the established Anglo-Jews backed the Government, with Chief Rabbi, J H Hertz calling those who refused to enlist 'laggards';[11] Jewish trade unionists, socialists and anarchists, like Milly, resisted. As Milly's anti-war protests escalated, she was arrested. In court, she was encouraged by her lawyer to renounce her actions. She refused. She was sentenced to two and half years, but the judge commented on her honesty and courage.[12]

The feminist cause

After two years in prison, Milly was released. She left London with Fermin to join Rudolph, who'd been deported to the Netherlands in a

Red Cross prisoner exchange agreement. In November 1918, they all moved to Berlin.

Despite their stint in prison, the revolutionary couple continued their fight. In 1919, they helped form Freie Arbeiter Union Deutschland (FAUD), which translates as Free Workers' Union Germany. The group embraced anarcho-syndicalism, which draws on anarchist traditions. It views unionism as a method for workers to gain control of an economy and influence broader society. The aim was to abolish the wage system, and dismantle any form of hierarchy that couldn't be ethically justified. Their main idea was: power corrupts.

While Milly was central to the formation of FAUD, it remained a male dominated organisation that overlooked women's issues. It became clear that the women needed to organise autonomously. From the start, Milly was the engine driving this forward. The founding of the Women's Union in Greater Berlin was mostly her initiative. The Union adopted principals of anarcho-syndicalism, but from a feminist perspective. It recognised the double burden for women – that of a worker and a woman. Today we'd call it intersectionality.

The Union took up issues facing housewives and mothers, actively organising with them. Milly established a children's group, arranged leisure activities, and advocated for youth welfare. Birth control became a key concern, including access to sex education, abortion and contraception. She argued it was the only way women would gain economic liberation. She called for a 'birth strike', arguing for bodily autonomy for women; a position she established some sixty years before the Women's Liberation Movement made it their own.

Recognising that housewives and mothers couldn't organise within a union, she encouraged them to use their economic influence. While men staged strikes in their workplace, she urged women to organise consumer boycotts. She demanded work in the home be treated equally to employment, encouraging collective female power to exert influence. Recognising the double burden of work and home for employed women, she advocated for the use of electrical household appliances to reduce housework hours.

Milly opposed marriage, calling it the 'deepest cause of women's slavery'. She and Rudolph never married. In fact, earlier in their relationship they'd tried to emigrate to the US for work, but were refused entry due to being unmarried. They were accused of advocating free love, to which Milly replied: 'Love is always free. When love ceases to be free it is prostitution.'[13]

Fighting fascism

Parallel to her feminist causes, she fought against racism and fascism. The anti semitism that came to power in Germany in 1933 with the National Socialists, alarmed Milly and Rudolph. They were equally as shocked by the indifference from workers and unions. Following the Reichstag fires, it became more than an organising concern. They fled to the USA. When WW2 broke out, in a radical change of position, Milly gave her support to the allied cause. She didn't believe pacifism alone could defeat the Nazis.

While Milly would never return to Europe, she continued to support comrades there. With Rudolph, she launched a publicity campaign to educate Americans about revolutionary events in Spain. After the war, she provided material support to German anarchists who'd survived the Nazi regime. It became her key focus during the post war years, raising money through the Jewish community in the US.

This would be her final act of solidarity. In early 1955, her health began to fail. Plagued by a series of illnesses, she recovered but was left weakened. She complained of feeling tired all the time, and had difficulty breathing. In November 1955, age 78, she passed away. Rudolph wrote: 'She died as she lived – brave, composed and without complaint'.[14]

News of her death spread rapidly all over the world. Messages of condolence came from almost every country: old friends, trade unions, libertarian groups and other organisations. Rudolph said: 'We have all lost her, for, with Milly, one of the last of the old guard has passed away, one who contributed 60 years of her life to a cause that will never die as long as men live on this earth.'[15]

Her legacy

Milly lived through an era of multiple conflicts, which devastated the Jewish community. Like many Jews of the era, she repeatedly fled persecution. Yet she didn't cower in the shadows. She remained passionate and committed to her principals, even facing prison for the cause. She lived her truth to the fullest extent of her abilities.

Through tireless campaigning, she politicised the field of reproduction, bringing it into the consciousness of men. She hacked away at the hierarchical separation between public and private life, creating spaces for women to help themselves. She legitimised their struggles, which were overlooked by so many.

What strikes me most about Milly is how ahead of her time she was about body autonomy, laying the foundations for the Women's Liberation Movement in the 70s and 80s. She was consciousness raising decades before second wave feminists, and advocating for reproductive justice long before Gloria Steinem put on a pair of aviator glasses. Her tireless work created a pathway to securing abortion rights in the twentieth century. It even has echoes for trans women fighting for better health care today.

In an essay written after her death, Rudolph claimed they were inseparable; that those around them could not mention one without the other. Sadly, history has forced them apart. While Rudolph's name lives on, with his work often quoted in traditional historical texts, Milly is largely forgotten. She clings on through a short Wikipedia page, but Rudolph's is at least five times longer. Her role in the 1912 strikes is completely airbrushed from history. I only discovered her amazing act of solidarity in supporting the children of the striking dock workers, through Rudolph's personal accounts. If she was, as Rudolph claims, not someone who did things by half measures, we can only assume she was more involved, especially as she'd worked in the tailoring sweatshops in London. Yet if she was more involved, her precise actions are lost to time.

Rudolph claimed that she was as important and influential as him, yet she's not held the same space in history. Like other women of revolutionary spirit – Eleanor Marx, May Morris, Margaret McDonald[16] – history forces her to live in the shadows of the men around her. Yet narratives are changing, as we retrieve more women from the dustbin of history. Ada Lovelace now claims her rightful place as a computer pioneer (although she is depressingly still referred to as Bryon's daughter, even though she never met him). Milly unfortunately has the added burden of being poor and an immigrant. It's time we lifted her up again; to give her the place in history she deserves.

Chapter 3

Adelaide Rise Up!

This chapter has descriptions of child abuse, suicide and sexual assault. Please take care while reading.

At 8am, Thomas Knight set off down the stone cobbled streets of Bow, not far from where the match woman would soon have their infamous strike. The place was already bustling, with a smell of horse manure in the air, and barefooted children in ragged clothes running through fetid puddles. Rats scurried amongst rubbish piled up on crowded streets. From passersby, he caught the brogue of Irish immigrants who'd fled the potato famine, no doubt heading to the docks to seek work. Reaching his hair salon, he prepared for another busy day. He'd be there until 10.30pm, as he had every other day that week.

It was a time of great political upheaval. The Peterloo massacre was within in living memory, and the Chartist movement in full swing. A few years earlier, Marx and Engels wrote The Communist Manifesto; and three years before that Engels wrote The Condition of the Working Class in England. Thomas probably hadn't read either as he was most likely illiterate, but his salon was a place where people came to discuss these ideas. On Saturdays, he shut at noon, and the discussion went to the beer and alehouses, with some gambling thrown in for fun. He'd be back at work Sunday morning, no doubt nursing a hangover.

In 1853, Thomas married Francis Attercliffe. She ran a tailoring business from home, and between them they eked out a modest lifestyle. That same year their first son was born, who they called Thomas. Frances continued to work from home, juggling business with childcare. Five more children followed, all of them daughters. The last to arrive was little Adelaide in 1871. By this time the household was far less happy.

Thomas' habit of drinking and gambling had spiralled, and he sunk further into debt as his business declined. Any reproach from Frances was met with violence. In one particularly cavalier gamble, he lost the entire salon and was forced into general labouring. As money became tighter, tensions in the household grew. Pregnant with Adelaide, Frances feared for the life of her unborn child. Leaving the children with a cousin in Bethnal Green, she fled to Devon.

Adelaide was born on 25th November 1871. Most noticeable at the time of her birth was her deformed hands – both her thumbs curved. Thomas was distraught when he heard, believing it a curse or grim predictor of the future. He begged Frances to return, vowing to stop drinking. She eventually agreed, a decision she later regretted.

Known as 'Dyddy', Adelaide was a happy child, with an outstanding memory, strong sense of drama and determination. Her unusual thumbs didn't seem to bother her much, any inconvenience quickly overcome. Yet by the time Adelaide was three years old, her father was back in the ale houses. Along with it came his violent temper.

One day, Dyddy was sent to the local shops to run some errands. When she arrived, the shop keeper was struggling to reach something that had fallen between a narrow gap. She asked little Adelaide if she could squeeze in and retrieve it. When she did, she found an old penny on the floor, which she handed to the shop keeper. She was rewarded with some sweets, which she shared with her friends playing outside.

One of the children had lost a penny, which had been given to her for her birthday. She accused Adelaide of stealing the money to buy the sweets, and fled home in distress. Other children took up the accusation, and the mother came out and confronted Adelaide. She was branded a liar, thief, and the child of a drunkard. Into this scene stumbled Thomas, vowing to cure Adelaide of her wicked ways. He ripped off his belt and beat her until she was unconscious. Alerted by the noise, the horrified shop keeper stepped in and verified Adelaide's story. Full of remorse, Thomas once again pledged sobriety, but his relationship with Adelaide never recovered.

School life

The year before Adelaide was born, landmark legislation introduced a national education system in England and Wales for the first time. Yet school was still not compulsory everywhere, and even where it was, it was poorly enforced. Many parents didn't see the point of educating girls, as the only ambition for them was marriage and babies. They'd be of more use at home, helping with chores or piecemeal work mothers took on to supplement the family income. So it is notable that Adelaide's parents bucked this trend, sending her to school with her brother. It may have been the importance they placed on education, or perhaps they'd noticed Adelaide's sharp mind.

It was on her way to school one day that Adelaide would suffer the first of a series of life changing incidents. While waiting for a friend, she climbed up on a wall. A large dog came by and barked at her ferociously. She fell off the wall in fright, and broke her back. She was taken to the Royal London Hospital in Whitechapel, where she spent several months lying in a plaster cast jacket. When she eventually returned home, she continued to wear a steal corset for support.

Following the accident, Thomas sank into a deep depression, blaming himself for the incident. He began drinking again, and the violence soon followed. One night, he returned from the pub, drunk as usual. As soon as he stepped into the house, he began to beat Frances. Adelaide jumped into protect her. Frances snatched her up, and they fled the house. She went to the police, requesting a summons for assault. That summons was served a week later, on 17th March 1879.

The evening of the summons, Thomas staggered into the house, coming face to face with Adelaide. She shrank from him. Seeing the terror in his child, he slumped to the floor, sobbing. He pleaded for her forgiveness. Then he ransacked the room, throwing documents from a drawer on to the floor. He found his marriage certificate and a razor, and began shredding. Testing the sharpness of the blade on his thumb, he held his arms out-stretched and said: 'Come Dyddy, come to Papa. We shall both have lovely red necklaces, won't that be nice.'[1] Adelaide fled behind some furniture. Thomas took a heavy curtain chord, tied it around his neck, and climbed on a chair. He once again asked for her forgiveness, then stepped off.

The second accident

Disaster for the family did not end there. Soon after, when Adelaide was only eight years old, she was running an errand for her mother. A mist fell, turning quickly into what Londoners called a 'pea souper' – a thick, often yellow or green fog, caused by air pollution. Crossing roads, she weaved in and out of people and traffic, but slipped on the cobbled stones. Unable to see in the gloom, a passing horse-drawn bus ran over her. She was rushed to hospital, and diagnosed with a fractured leg, ribs and badly damaged hip. Once again, she'd spend months in a cast.

Adelaide was forced to wear leg splints and walk with crutches. She remained in considerable pain. Returning to the hospital for further investigation, they discovered she had a diseased hip. She was confined to bed, and forbidden from using her left leg. Watching it wither from lack of use, she feared she may never walk again. She took matters into her own hands, secretly putting her leg on to the floor, stuffing bedsheets into her mouth to stop from screaming at the pain. Each day she increased the amount of pressure she put on it. To the surprise of her family and doctors, the leg strengthened. Although it caused discomfort for the rest of her life, always needing a stick to walk with, Adelaide's courage and determination saved her leg.

Along comes Donald

By 1884, Frances' health had declined, plunging the family further into crisis. Having already moved to a smaller house a few years before, the family crammed themselves into one room, renting the other out to a lodger. It was older brother Tom, who introduced them to Donald Adolphus Brown, a merchant seaman in need of lodgings. Born in 1873 in Sheerness in Kent, Donald's father was originally from Ebini in what is now Gyana. Little is known about his mother. Donald followed his father's passion for ships, spending most of his young adult life at sea.

The minute he and Adelaide met, they struck up a rapport. They bonded over their religious connection, love of singing, and reading and discussing political ideas. They were motivated by the match women strike, and the plight of the working classes.

Frances loved Donald too, but not everyone in the family did. In 1894, when Adelaide and Donald announced they would marry, her older sisters accused her of bringing shame on to the family for marrying a black man. They even got her doctor to intervene, who told Donald that if he married Adelaide he should be 'prepared to bury her.' Donald was incensed, and told the doctor: 'Sir, if Adelaide will marry me we will find some happiness together. When and if that time comes it will be my privilege to bury her.'[2]

The marriage went ahead. Once again breaking with convention, Adelaide saw no reason to take Donald's name, and he saw no need to insist. Their approach to the home was also radical. Seeing how much pain Adelaide was in, Donald took on every task he could to relieve her burden. That included washing, cooking and shopping. They sang together to keep their spirits up, and on good days Donald made sandwiches and they would picnic in the park.

But racism was never far from their door. In 1895, their first child was born. Donald had left Adelaide and the baby sleeping to tell her Aunt Betsy the good news. While he was out, a drunken neighbour broke into their home. Making her way to the bedroom, she pulled the covers from the baby's cot, screaming: 'Let's see this black bastard.'[3] She jumped on the bed and sexually assaulted Adelaide, causing her to haemorrhage. The sight of so much blood shocked the woman, and she fled from the house, leaving behind an unconscious mother and crying baby. The baby's cries brought in a neighbour, who immediately called the midwife. Rumours spread, and an angry mob gathered around Adelaide's home, believing she'd been raped by her black husband. When Donald returned, threats, jeers and stones were thrown at him. Aunt Betsy rushed him into the house to escape the murderous crowd. For days after, Adelaide hovered between life and death. Donald stayed by her side, slowly nursing her back to health.

A political education

In 1897, Adelaide fell pregnant again. Concerned about the impact on her health, Donald retired from the high seas. He took temporary labouring jobs, before finding work in a munitions factory in Woolwich. During this time, there was huge growth in the establishment of public libraries, including in working class areas. Like many others, Donald used them to educate himself, along with enrolling in evening classes. With Adelaide, they questioned the truth that was presented to them, challenged injustice and ignorance, and examined their religious beliefs and convictions. Motivated by her experiences with her father, Adelaide was heavily involved in the temperance movement. As her worldview grew, this made way for something larger.

The women's movement

The WSPU was led primarily by Emmeline Pankhurst, and her eldest daughter Christabel. In the earliest days of the organisation, Christabel couldn't take on the role her mother envisaged, as she was finishing her law degree. So Emmeline assigned her middle daughter, Sylvia, the role of honorary secretary. A committed socialist, Sylvia wanted to develop links between the suffrage and labour movements. In 1892, former miner, Kier Hardy had won the parliamentary seat of West Ham South as an independent candidate. The following year he helped form the Independent Labour Party (ILP). So Sylvia dispatched fellow suffragette, Annie Kenney, to East London, where she visited local ILP branches to met women labour rights activists. In 1906, they set up the first branch of the WSPU in Canning Town, West Ham. Adelaide was there at once, becoming the branch secretary.

During her time at the WSPU, Adelaide spoke at meetings about the problems experienced by working class women, including poverty, back street abortions and sweated labour. That same year, Adelaide formed part of a delegation that went to Herbert Asquith's house, a prominent member of the Liberal Party. They attempted to secure a meeting, but their request was refused. Unwilling to accept the rejection, Annie Kenney began ringing the doorbell. The police were called, and violently dragged the women away. On 4th July 1906, Adelaide and two other women appeared at Marylebone Court, and were sentenced to six weeks in prison unless they agreed to behave themselves, and give up campaigning. It was a difficult decision for Adelaide, who was in poor health and now had two small children, the youngest only 18 months old. In a letter to Donald, Adelaide wrote: 'What can I do Daddy? To draw back will encourage this intimidation. Can I count on your full support? It will be agonising to be away from you and our children, but with your help I can face this.'[4]

There were many offers of help to look after the children, especially from the wealthier women. There was even an offer to adopt the baby, which was firmly rejected. In the end, Donald stepped up with his full support, saying: 'My dear Mamma, we have supported each other for many years [...] we must not fail now that we are put to the test'[5] Adelaide knew with her husband by her side she could face anything, so headed to Holloway prison to face whatever would come.

On arrival at Holloway, the women were ordered to undress. They were given coarse dresses, and sent to a dirty cell. A hard-faced warden told them to scrub it clean. It was a job they were instructed to perform every morning, causing Adelaide great pain due to having to kneel on the damp floor.

Conditions in the prison were dire. They found rats dropping in their food and the screams of other women kept them awake at night. Yet Adelaide tackled her incarceration with determination and resilience. Every morning she'd sing the socialist anthem, The Red Flag, scratching its lyrics into the window of her cell with a hairpin. In a letter to Donald, she wrote: 'I may tell you that I am far from downhearted. If it becomes necessary they will find that members of the Women's Social and Political Union are willing to forgo their liberty and return to the place again and again, until we receive our political freedom.'[6]

On their release, a lively ceremonial committee met the three suffragettes at the gates. They were driven in an open top car, with a sign attached that read, Asquith's Prisoners. While fellow members of the WSPU cheered them on, there were jeers from some passersby. As the campaign escalated, the WSPU gave medals to activists who'd sacrificed their liberty. As one of the earliest pioneers, this tradition had perhaps not started at the time of Adelaide's incarceration, as there's no evidence she received one.

Adelaide's stay at Holloway took its toll, and she returned a weakened woman. The joy of being back with her family helped her through the pain, and within in a few weeks she was back in the thick of the fight, organising groups of East End women to go around London as needed. Her ability to organise was noticed, and she was recruited to the WSPU central committee. Yet a huge betrayal was around the corner.

On 15th December 1906, fellow suffragette, Dora Montifore wrote to Adelaide, expressing her concern about a policy being pursued by the WSPU central committee. In the letter she said that in order to do a deal with the Tories, the WSPU leaders would bargain for an agreement that gave women who paid taxes the vote. This would exclude most working class women. They wanted universal suffrage. Dora wrote: 'It makes me heartsick to see what is going on and to know that the working women are going to be betrayed by their leaders just as working men have been betrayed over and over again.'[7]

Unlike Sylvia, Emmeline and Christabel Pankhurst hadn't wanted to link the suffrage campaign with the labour movement. They believed in campaigning for the vote as a single issue; they thought anything else was a distraction. In fact, Christabel was not interested in working class involvement at all, calling for only the 'strongest and most intelligent' to be involved.[8]

Back at her branch in West Ham, Adelaide hammered home that only unity would bring justice to all women. They agreed to write a letter to Kier Hardy asking for his support for working class women. The WSPU central committee was informed of their actions.

On her way to the next central committee meeting, Adelaide was held up and had to squeeze in at the back of the room. She listened, dumbfounded, as Christabel Pankhurst made the most amazing speech. She said she'd been with Kier Hardy when he opened the letter, and claimed he'd 'wept bitter tears to think how misguided these poor souls were'. He agreed that an educated leadership must show them the correct way.[9] All eyes turned to Adelaide, who was speechless. On her way to the meeting, she'd met her cousin Joe, who she'd given the letter to a week before. He apologised; he'd been busy, and the letter had never been posted.

She gathered her composure and stood up, announcing to the crowd: 'Ladies, I am sure that members of my branch will be dismayed and desperately unhappy to feel that we caused our beloved Kier Hardy to shed bitter tears … over a letter, which ladies, he never did receive.' She held up the sealed letter.[10]

There was dismay, indignation and sorrow when Adelaide reported back to the West Ham branch. The more militant members condemned the behaviour of the central committee, while others struggled to accept there'd been such dishonesty. Meanwhile, changes were mounting at a pace within the central committee. Having finished her education, Christabel took the reins, and began cutting ties with all political parties, including the ILP. Where once the suffragettes marched with red socialist flags, these were replaced with the purple, green and white sash that we know so well today. In West Ham, Adelaide resigned her position of branch secretary. It closed shortly after, complaining of neglect by the leaders of the movement.

Over the next few years all East London branches of the WSPU closed. They never re-established them. The political drive of women in this radical part of the capital lived on though. Sylvia Pankhurst returned to Bow in 1914 and establish the ELFS. Meanwhile, Adelaide was invited by Dora Montefiore to travel with her to Paris, to speak with French suffragists. For a woman of her background to embark on such international travel must have felt like a huge adventure, yet the trip had massive consequences for her health. On her return she stepped back from activism although continued to write letters to the press on racism, poverty and the emancipation of women.

Escape to the country

In 1909, Adelaide gave birth once more, and her health deteriorated even further. With mixed feelings, the family left the East End for Abbey Wood, which at the time was part of Kent but now lies in the London Borough of Greenwich. Their political discussions continued, and Donald remained active in the trade union at his munitions factory. Adelaide joined the Cooperative Women's Guild, and they both continued their membership of the ILP, often bringing their children along to meetings.

In 1917, Adelaide was moved by events in Russia and the sacrifices of the Russian people. Inspired by the solidarity of the workers and their determination to defend the land, in 1919 she joined the Communist Party of Great Britain. During the 1921–22 Russian famine, Adelaide and Donald helped raise funds for their comrades, and opened their home to those seeking refuge from the authorities. As suspicions about communism grew, the couple found themselves the target of investigations, with their home searched by the Criminal Investigations Department (CID).

Adelaide was nominated as a possible delegate for a trip to the Soviet Union, organised by the Women's Cooperative Guild. But her health was too poor for travel. She'd hoped that her daughter Winifred would follow in her footsteps, but from around the age of eight, she was a full time carer for her frail mother. In 1949, Adelaide passed away aged 78 years old. Donald died the following year.

Adelaide's legacy

On 20th June 1914, six women walked into 10 Downing Street to meet with Herbert Asquith, who was now Prime minister. Delegations of suffragettes were nothing new, but this was the first time a group of working class women had gone, organised by the ELFS. The six told of their hard lives and the tough working conditions: Jessie Payne was a boot maker; Daisy Parsons was a cigarette packer; and Jane Savoy was a brush maker, all working long hours for little pay. Mrs Ford talked about sexual harassment at the clothing factory she worked at; Julia Scurr was a member of the Poplar Board of Poor Law Guardians. The story of Mrs Bird, the final delegate, is sadly lost to time.

Following the meeting with the East London suffragettes, Asquith is said to have been uncharacteristically moved by the delegation[11] and the New Statesmen suggested the PM's response marked a 'distinct step forward in the suffragette agitation'. Asquith himself said: 'If the change [women's suffrage] has got to come we must face it boldly and make it thoroughly democratic in its basis.'[12] Despite WSPU's insistence on the greater strength of rich women, Asquith was forced to negotiate by working class women from East London.[13]

It was early pioneers like Adelaide who laid the path for these women; with sacrifices of her liberty and health that showed extraordinary courage. Yet we may not have known about her at all if her daughter, Winifred, hadn't written her biography. Originally only intended as a story for the family, in 2007 her granddaughter, Fay Jacobsen, decided to publish it in case it may interest others. There are many more untold stories of working class suffragettes, who we should thank every time we go to the ballot box.

Chapter 4

Eva Rise Up!

Rising up from the lush marshes of the Lea Valley, on the edge of Epping's ancient woodlands, was the pretty village of Leyton. Until the coming of the railways in the mid-nineteenth century, it was a place where London's wealthy merchants and bankers built grand houses in which to retire. In 1840, the opening of Leabridge station, and later Low Leyton and Leytonstone, radically changed this rural landscape. The elite watched in horror as rows of yellow-bricked workers terrace houses went up. Their leafy retreat turned into a suburban dormitory for clerks and workman, who could commute quickly and cheaply into the East End.

For the workers it was liberation. Out of the cramped, smog filled streets of Spitalfields, they finally had entire homes. No squashing your entire family into one room; no more bugs in the walls, and cracks in the ceilings where rain came through; no more wrapping your dresses in brown paper to protect them from damp. What's more, the 1878 Epping Forest Act protected over 200 acres of trees, ponds, glades and open spaces, providing opportunities for outdoor recreation for the new residents.

With the growing population came schools, shops and libraries. In 1882, the first town hall was built, and in 1903, Whipps Cross Hospital. According to census data, in 1861 Leyton had a population of 10,394; rising to 27,068 by 1881. By 1911 it reached 124,735. It was no longer little leafy Leyton.

In 1903, 21-year-old Eva Slawson sat in one of these newly built workers' homes, writing a letter to her friend, Ruth Slate. They'd met at church, both girls from lower middle-class Nonconformist Methodist families. They were brought up to believe in the importance of respectable, honest labour, a commitment to their religion and responsibility towards family. Ruth's father was a commercial clerk, in precarious employment.

Eva was illegitimate, adopted by her grandparents. Her grandfather was a baker, who floated in and out of debt.

Both girls left school in their early teens, to contribute to the family wage. Ruth's first job was manual packing work, before progressing to a clerical job. Eva's grandmother encouraged her into domestic service with the Duke of Westminster. But the stress made her physical ill. When her grandparents were better off, she learnt shorthand and typing, securing new employment at Cartwright and Cunningham, a solicitor's in Walthamstow.

Eva and Ruth shared a frustration with religious doctrine, feeling there must be more to life. They longed for a mission that was noble and self-sacrificing; something more than years of dreary clerical labour. Yet these dreams were discouraged, particularly by Ruth's family. Such a cause required money, which neither of them had.

Yet the world around them was changing. In 1908, Eva joined the Leyton branch of the ILP. At her first meeting she felt out of place as a line of men filed into the hall. Of the 90 branch members, she was one of only 10 women. She found a more comfortable political home within the women's movement, which was turning Victorian society upside down. Eva and Ruth's letters and diaries[1] paint a vivid picture of this new generation, who wanted more from life than marriage and children.

Suffragettes

In June 1908, Ruth met Eva at Liverpool Street station. While on their way to Charing Cross, they saw a Votes for Women procession. In her diary[2], Ruth describes bands playing music, while thousands of women marched. They carried banners, large and small. The larger banners were 'exceedingly beautiful' representing great women from history, including George Elliot, Charlotte Bronte, Joan of Arc and Boudica. The smaller ones represented the different trades groups women belonged to, including clerks, typists, lace-makers, nurses and painters. The two friends watched the procession for an hour, while the crowds around them cheered and applauded. Ruth describe it as 'a most impressive sight.'

While inspired by the demonstration, Eva remained unimpressed with the militant tactics of WSPU. In 1911, she argued with her Aunt Edie, and half-sister Gertie over their decision to become militants. On 4th June 1913, the suffragette, Emily Wilding Davidson, fell under the King's horse on Derby Day, dying later of her injuries. On hearing the news, Eva responded with horror, writing in her diary[3]: 'I cannot express what a shock this news was to me – can such martyrdom and sacrifice really be necessary? Will it hasten the longed-for cause?' A short while later, she complained about the WSPU's publication, The Suffragette, and the off hand way it talked about militant actions, such as burning homes and wrecking paintings.

In 1907, the WSPU removed voting rights from its members. Decision making would now be the responsibility of a committee, hand picked by Emmeline Pankhurst. Many members were up in arms. Following a failed attempt to get the unconstitutional ruling overturned, a break away group formed. They called themselves the Women's Freedom League (WFL). They campaigned for the parliamentary vote using non-violent methods, such as demonstrations, chaining themselves to objects in the Houses of Parliament, non payment of taxes and refusal to complete the census.

In 1909, Eva wrote to Charlotte Despard, the president of the WFL, asking for advice on the best course of action to take for the women's cause. She received a 'helpful and sympathetic' reply. In 1913, she attended a WFL meeting with her Aunt Edie at Caxton Hall in Westminster. Afterwards, she wrote in her diary how at home she felt. She seemed enraptured by the meeting, describing Charlotte Despard's speech about love, while wearing 'a grey dress and scarf of heaven sent blue.' Afterwards there was a Hindu musician performing on an instrument she'd never seen before, while a young Indian girl danced. In what could be a hint at the future direction of her life, Eva exclaimed: 'I could have kissed every part of her – I felt intoxicated by the beauty of the human body, the joy of motion.'[4]

It's interesting that Eva threw her lot in with the WFL, rather than the ELFS like her half-sister Gertie. Like the WPSU, the WFL only campaigned for the vote on the same terms as men, which in 1913 wouldn't have included Eva. The ELFS meanwhile campaigned for universal suffrage, understanding economic freedom could only be won when everyone had a voice in the democratic process.

Female 'inverts'

Eva's social and political outlook grew following the publication of Edward Carpenter's Love's Coming of Age. This short series of essays on gender roles explored the spectrum of sexual identities, acceptance of open relationships and the stifling nature of traditional marriage. Carpenter was an advocate for women's liberation, and equality between the sexes. While he still saw women as sexually passive, he argued that 'deviant' forms of sexuality were not a moral problem, but a medical one. He believed that female 'inverts' (the word lesbian wasn't in popular usage) were a naturally occurring type of women, for whom a female body enclosed a masculine soul and temperament. While still far from modern perceptions of sexuality, it was radical for its time.

Carpenter's work made a significant impact on many people, including Kathlyn Oliver, founder of the Domestic Workers' Union. Kathlyn had called off two previous marriage engagements. After reading Carpenter's work, she wrote to him declaring herself a 'urning', the historic term for homosexual. In 1909, she publicly came out by writing a letter to the Women Worker, stating 'I have been more in love with women than I have with any of the opposite sex.' She would go on to place a number of lonely hearts ads in the newspaper, seeking female relationships.[5]

Carpenter's work also had a big influence on Eva. She wrote to Ruth, describing the book as, 'full of suggestion and as I read my mind wanders off along various lines'. She went on to say, 'my views on marriage are altering to an alarming extent – I really believe some people would call my opinions immoral!'[6]

Despite these radical ideas about relationships, Eva still appeared to believe that marriage and motherhood was the ideal for women. She seemed plagued by a sense of loss and complained, 'single women are "outside the heart of things", our friendship with happily married men and women after all only touches the fringes of their lives."[7]

Eva used her diaries and letters to Ruth to reflect on political theories, and the role of women in society. In Feb 1913[8], she describes an incident at the solicitor's firm where she worked, involving a 19-year-old woman. She had given birth to an illegitimate child, which plunged her into crisis 'her nerves having completely given away'. Pursing legal justice, Mr Cunningham interviewed the father, 'a bold, coarse faced youth who denies the charges'. They argued, with raised voices, before the man abruptly left, singing 'I don't care what becomes of me'. Eva pondered in her journal on whether this was true, or bravado. She wrote: 'It is hard to understand why so much physical, mental and spiritual suffering should fall to the lot of women in these cases.'

Meeting Minna

In 1911, Eva met Minna Simmons, an older, married women. Their meeting left an impression on Eva, who described Minna as 'the type of woman of the future – maternal, calm, sensitive, spiritual and strong […] she interests me exceedingly'[9] From 1913 onwards, Eva spent more time in the 'warm and affectionate' atmosphere of Minna's home, and her 'unconventional social and political views'.[10] Minna was married to Will, and they had three teenage children – Winnie, Edie and Horace. In June 1913, Minna became pregnant with her fourth, aged 40.

In early 1914, Will fell ill with consumption and was sent away to a sanatorium. Sadly, on 4th February he died. Eva went immediately to Minna, and shortly after moved in. Their conversations became more intimate, discussing passion, sensuality and sexual union. On 6th March, Minna's baby was born

In her diary, Eva describes sleeping in Minna's arms on many occasions. There was clearly an erotic dimension to this physical intimacy. She wrote: 'Such waves of love pass through me at times. I quiver with feeling'[11] and '(t)onight in bed it seems our very souls and bodies mingled in love and sympathy.'[12] Although not an explicit reference to sexual interaction, that wouldn't be an unreasonable interpretation.

Yet the birth of Minna's baby aroused complex emotions in Eva. She wrote in her diary of a longing for a child, which triggered a great sadness. She scolded herself for wanting to stay away from Minna when jealousy of motherhood arose. Meanwhile, Ruth read Eva a poem by Edward Carpenter about urnings and the intermediate sex. They discussed the possibility of such women having children, but became muddled in the complexity of the ideas.

War, pacifism and the Quakers

By mid-1914, war had shattered everyday life. The women's movement was further split when Emmeline and Christabel Pankhurst stopped campaigning, throwing their energies into the war effort. Meanwhile, many of the women Eva admired, including Charlotte Despard, opposed the conflict.

A few months earlier, Ruth secured a scholarship to study at Woodbrooke Settlement, a Quaker institution for religious and social study. In this atmosphere, she quickly joined the pacifist movement promoted by the Quakers. Eva also took a pacifist stance, despite the risks. She wrote in her diary about the limiting opportunities for women who didn't support the war effort.

Meanwhile, Eva's sister Gertie became more involved with the ELFS, who turned their attentions to the economic hardships created by war. While initially the factories closed down due to lack of workers, a mass recruitment of women allowed them to reopen again. However, they paid women a fraction of the men's wages. On average, a factory owner would employ three women for the one man who'd left for the frontline. Yet the women had the same hungry mouths to feed. Sylvia Pankhurst embarked on an energetic letter writing campaign to Prime Minister, Lloyd George. Her fellow suffragettes marched on Whitehall, demanding equal work for equal pay. In 1915, the government finally agreed to pay women the same piece rate as men – the same price for each item produced. Yet it was only a partial win, as the factory owners simply moved to hourly rates to get around the legislation. Around this time, Eva switched from reading The Suffragette, the WPSU newspaper, to The Dreadnought, the ELFS publication. She described it as extremely interesting.

Eva began attending Quaker meetings with Ruth. She was inspired by a call to support German immigrants in Britain, many of whom, like Rudolph Rocker, faced prejudice or internment as enemy aliens. Excited by this internationalist approach, she vowed to suggest it at her own church.

During this time, a relationship blossomed between Eva and Mr James, a minister at her church. One evening, he invited her over to discuss their relationship. He declared the strength of his feelings towards her, and Eva returned home in a 'state of ecstasy'.[13] Yet she complained his manner was too formal, and believed he could benefit from lessons from Whitman and Carpenter, both known for their radical approach to sexuality. In the end, Eva's relationship with Mr James fizzled out as she accepted a scholarship for Woodbrooke, which Ruth helped secure.

Life at Woodbrooke

It took time for Eva to settle into Woodbrooke, as she was less used to socialising than Ruth, battling depression and low self-confidence. She eventually found her feet, attending 'no conscription' meetings run by the Quakers, where conscientious objectors were discussed. Eva supported exemption from military service on conscience grounds, a radical position that put her at odds with the general public.

On 27th February 1916, Eva wrote to Ruth about her new friends, who were opening up new worlds to her. They described their work in Nottingham, training and educating young women in 'needlework, cookery and debates', while encouraging them to organise within the workplace for their rights. Eva wrote that 'if I cannot get work within the Labour or Cooperative movements, I really think I would like this kind of work.'[14]

Her letter is interrupted by a terrible headache. It was the last she sent to Ruth, as a week later she died from undiagnosed diabetes. This was no doubt the cause of the headache, due to other symptoms she mentions throughout her diary, including tiredness and leg pain. She died on the brink of the new life she'd desired for so long.

After Eva

The sudden and unexpected death of Eva devastated both Ruth and Minna. In her diary Ruth wrote. 'Friendship has been the breath of life and Eva my crown […] I was so sure that she had special work to do in this world and I used to picture myself as her righthand helper.'[15]

Ruth and Minna grew closer, bonded by their sorrow. Minna wrote a number of letters to Ruth, in which she described the intensity of their friendship, and seemed to suggest she saw it in sexual terms. She wrote: 'How I pray dear earnestly for God to take away my intense longing for her, sometimes it seems just too much to bear […] I will tell you of my thoughts on the intermediate sex another time.'[16] and a few weeks later: 'I am going to be daring and write and speak on the sex questions. I <u>will</u>. I <u>will</u>.'[17] Sadly there are no extant letters containing Minna's thoughts.

Eva's legacy

While Eva didn't live to fulfil her potential, she was part of a movement that did. The suffragettes are best known for their fight for equal suffrage, but their challenge of social norms and expectations of women's behaviour shouldn't be ignored. The suffragettes, more than any other group, represented the new woman movement. They sought financial independence, expanded social roles, and rejected marriage and motherhood in return for supportive relationships with other women. Some formed female residential communities, which provided alternative domestic structures. Love may have been encouraged within the all-female environment and anti-male ethos, and they certainly had a more fluid attitude to female friendships.[18]

Our current definitions of lesbianism and bi-sexuality are historically specific. At the turn of the last century there wasn't a vocabulary or clear definition for women to define themselves; if indeed they even wanted to. As Martha Vicinus says in the Lesbian and Gay Studies Reader: 'We must accept a confusing and fragmented history.'[19]

There are many notable examples of this incomplete history. Dr Louisa Martindale, suffragist and pioneer in women's health, never married and lived for three decades with Ismay FitzGerald. Louisa wrote in her 1951 autobiography, openly (although not explicitly), about her feelings for Ismay, saying 'I have had my full share of love and happiness.'

Socialist and artist, May Morris, married Henry Sparling, a friend of her father's, William Morris. It's said she had an affair with George Bernard Shaw, and New York lawyer, John Quinn. It's her relationship with Mary Lobb that's garnered most interest recently. Mary worked on a farm opposite Kelmscott Manor, where May lived. She was short and stocky, drove a steam roller, wore knickerbockers and behaved in a manner not deemed appropriate for a woman. A strong relationship blossomed between Mary and May, spending time together at Kelmscott and travelling around Britain and Iceland. It's said that those around them didn't know what to make of the relationship.[20] But neighbourhood gossip and driving a steam roller is not sufficient evidence to label these women as queer.

Nor is a copy of abridged poems by Walt Whitman, inscribed 'the dear love of comrades', a phrase widely interpreted as a celebration of physical love between people of the same sex. The book was given to Emily Wilding-Davidson, from fellow suffragette, Mary Leigh. Their relationship was clearly close – Mary was a pallbearer at Emily's funeral – but that was not uncommon between women in the era. Known as romantic friendships, women often formed close bonds due to the social restrictions and stifling moral atmosphere.

Eva was an ordinary working-class woman from East London, but her dairies are important because of the insight they provide into same sex relationships during this period. While not explicitly stating the nature of their relationship, they are one of the strongest pieces of evidence we have. Without the language to describe their union, it's impossible for us to know without doubt. Yet they were certainly living outside gender norms, challenging the hetero-normative expectations of society.

Part II

1920–1939

Chapter 5

Minnie Rise Up!

It was a brutal February in 1889, with stormy weather and temperatures dropping well below freezing. Pulling up the collars of their coats, pale men roamed the dark streets looking for work. They'd arrived in the East End from around the world, fleeing persecution and hunger, only to find further want and hardship. The previous summer, tensions exploded at the match factory in Bow. As discontent mixed into the sweat of the dockers, gas workers, jam makers and tailors, they looked to those young women and made their own plans.

In the midst of this atmosphere of rebellion, a baby girl was born to a Jewish family on a damp street in Spitalfields, just behind Truman's Brewery. The homes around the Brewery were considered poor but respectable, inhabited by a mix of Irish and Jewish immigrants. According to Charles Booth's poverty maps, children looked 'clean' and 'well fed'[1]. Although not the worst of the East End slums, they were still overcrowded, with families of up to six all living in one room. From 4am, the neighbourhood woke from the noise of the steam engines that powered the brewing process. The smell of hops mixed with hay and manure, from draught horses who pulled wagons filled with barrels of beer. As the foreman yelled instructions, the drivers set off to deliver their goods across London and beyond.

On 9th February 1889, this hustle and bustle passed Issac and Annie Glassman by, as they held their new baby daughter in their arms. This was their second child, the first born a couple of years before. They called her Minnie, which has many different meanings in Hebrew. The most prophetic being rebel.

Issac Glassman was born in the Russian Empire, in what's now Poland. Like many other Jews facing state sponsored persecution, he came to

London in the mid-1880s with his new wife Hannah (known as Annie). Little is known about Minnie's mother, although it's probable that she was busy in the home, looking after her husband and what would end up being seven children. Issac found work as a bootmaker, which was a common trade for Jewish immigrants. Like other sweated trades, hours were long, wages poor and Charles Booth described the working conditions as 'huddled misery'.[2]

Before Minnie was a year old, the family moved to Newsman's Buildings on Pelham Street, where they took in a lodger to help pay the rent. This was the area known for the Jack the Ripper murders less than two years before. These horrors put pressure on the authorities to install gas lights, so the once dingy streets were at least a little brighter.

The family didn't remain here long, moving to Cricksand Street, which ran off Brick Lane. The area was dominated by Jews, with tailors, bootmakers and a synagogue. Booth described the population as 'respectable hardworking people on the whole.' The Glassman family called this home for the next 30 years.

School life

Minnie and her siblings attended Cricksand Elementary school, which was on the east side of their street. By the time Minnie reached school age, education was compulsory and free up to the age of 10. While boys and girls were educated together, they didn't learn the same things. Boys were taught with the expectation they'd enter the workforce; girls were drilled on duties of the home.

Just before her eighth birthday, Minnie transferred to the Jews' Free School on Bell Lane in Whitechapel. Established in 1732, it provided an education to the children of Jewish migrants in the East End. As Jews continued to flee persecution in the Russian empire, it became the largest Jewish school in Europe.

Boys and girls were kept separate, and again with different curriculums. Minnie learnt knitting and laundry work, and the best way to wash different fabrics. While Yiddish was the predominant language in most Jewish homes, a desire to assimilate meant they taught English in the classroom.

In 1899, the compulsory school age was raised to 12. So when Minnie turned 13 in 1902, she was no longer legally required to attend. There was huge pressure on working class girls to terminate their education, and either find work or help out in the home. Yet Minnie won a scholarship and continued her education at Coburn School for Girls. It's not clear why her parents allowed her to continue in school. By this point, her father had quit boot making and was working as a coal merchant. Perhaps the extra money gave them more flexibility; perhaps they spotted Minnie's intelligence; perhaps like many migrant families they recognised the importance of education. Maybe all of the above.

While government regulations still required girls to learn household skills, added to Minnie's curriculum was English literature, language and composition; modern languages; chemistry; art and maths. In order to keep her scholarship, Minnie was required to meet rigorous academic standards. She didn't fail. At 16, she passed her Junior Cambridge University Local Examinations, and won a school prize.[3]

Teaching and trade unions

Upon leaving elementary education, options for girls were limited. She may have found work in domestic service, at a factory, or piece work at home, producing match boxes or other small items. Minnie's advanced education opened up additional opportunities, but the choice was still narrow. Clerical work or teaching were the most common professions. Minnie opted for the later.

Since 1846, girls had learnt to teach primarily through the pupil-teacher system. At 13, teachers selected the brightest pupils, and they served a five-year apprenticeship in the classroom. The method was criticised for inadequate training and poor professional standards. The National Union of Teachers (NUT) called for proper qualifications, and blacklisting those who had none. In 1890, six training colleges opened at universities, and four more the following year. By 1900, there were 16 with 1150 students. The profession finally had academic status.[4]

Minnie was the first generation to go through this new system. In 1908, she took up a teacher training place at Goldsmiths College in New Cross. Although men and women studied together, there were a number of gender inequalities: women received a grant of £25 per year, while men received £30; men who lodged at the college had a curfew of 10pm, while women had to be home at 8pm; and women found certain areas out of bounds, designated for the male students only.[5]

Once qualified, things didn't get much better. While women teachers had a level of education and professional status on a par with men, full career rewards were not delivered. Compared to men, they had lower salaries, poorer promotional prospects, and a marriage bar restricting their employment.

In 1911, Minnie began working at Fairclough Street Elementary School in Whitechapel and immediately felt these injustices. While her wage was £90 per year, the men got £5 more. Unable to accept this, she went to the most obvious place for support – her union.

Minnie joined the NUT, and its local branch, the East London Teacher's Association (ELTA). In December 1913, she successfully proposed that the ELTA debate a resolution, for the NUT conference, supporting equal pay between men and women teachers. She lost by one vote.[6] Frustrated by the union, Minnie turned her attention to the broader women's struggle.

East London's suffragettes

In 1913, the WSPU stepped up its militancy. Many East London suffragettes felt uneasy with this escalation. If they went to prison they knew they would be more harshly treated. Teachers also felt cautious. If arrested, they could bring their profession into disrepute, or lose their jobs. These concerns were justified. In 1910, a teacher from Deptford was reprimanded for missing work to attend a women's suffrage demonstration, and later lost her job when she was sent to prison.

So while the WSPU leaders smashed windows and fire-bombed post boxes, the ELFS focused on collective action, such as rent strikes, outdoor meetings and large-scale demonstrations. Meanwhile, Poplar Borough Council had banned pro-suffragette meetings in its venues. It suggested it might be willing to revoke the ban if the women agreed to not make militant speeches, but they refused. When the Labour minority on the council challenged the ban, the Tory/Liberal majority refused to even discuss it. Enraged members of the public stormed the council chambers, throwing bags of yellow and blue powder over the councillors, tipping over ink stands and water bottles. The mayor adjourned the meeting, and the suffragettes sang songs and made speeches.[7]

Over the following months, Labour kept up the pressure to overturn the ban. Leading the charge was a young up-and-coming politician called Edgar Lansbury. He was about to change Minnie's life.

Along came Edgar

On a bench in Victoria park, sometime around 1906, Edgar and Minnie leaned in for their first kiss. Their relationship was full of passion, brought together by their dedication to social justice. Edgar was a handsome man: almost six foot tall, with broad shoulders and thick, dark, slightly unruly hair. He was described by fellow Poplar councillor, George Creswell, as 'a most loveable young man, and a splendid specimen of a man.'[8]

Edgar was the fifth chid of Bessie and George Lansbury, a social reformer and British politician, who'd go on to lead the Labour Party between 1932–35. In 1887, when Edgar was born, George was still a rank-and-file member of the Liberal Party, while working in Issac Brine's timber business. Disappointed in the party's lukewarm support for women's rights, he quit and joined the Social Democratic Federation (SDF), alongside Eleanor Marx, William Morris and Henry Hyman. By 1903 he'd become disenchanted with the SDF over Hyman's inability to work with other socialist groups. He joined the ILP, and was elected on to Poplar Borough Council. During his tenure he fought for reform of the poor laws and an end to the harsh workhouse system, for better housing and against sweated labour. In 1912, he founded the socialist newspaper, the Daily Herald.[9]

Once again, the stories of women are lost in the dust, so we know little about Edgar's mother, Bessie. We get a peek into her life from Edgar's writings:

> Father writes of the long week-ends spent away from his home. There were also the long evenings after work during which mother wrestled with a difficult and sometimes turbulent family, with father miles away lecturing and debating on Socialism and public affairs generally, or sitting for hours on committees and councils fighting the battles of the poor.[10]

It didn't go unnoticed that while George was fighting for the emancipation of women, he'd forgotten about the freedoms of his own wife. Yet she raised her daughters to aspire for more, and they became 'extremely intelligent, independent and forceful women.'[11]

Meanwhile, young Edgar attended his local school in Poplar, going on to secure a place at Kings College London. After graduating, he took a job in the civil service, but in 1910, he left his post to take over running the timber business, which his father had since inherited from Issac Brine. In 1912, Edgar stood for election to Poplar Council as a Labour representative, and won.

There was often huge pressure for Jewish girls to find a 'nice Jewish boy', which Edgar was not. Minnie's family may have been more liberal than most, as there's no record of them disapproving the match. There were other social pressures to face. Like other local authorities, London County Council (LCC) required women teachers to give up their careers when they married. We can only imagine the mental struggle Minnie went through – the career she'd worked so hard for, and won against the odds; or the man she loved. This might explain why there were eight years between that first kiss, and wedding bells. On 9th April 1914, they finally tied the knot at the Poplar registry office.

War widows and pensions

A few months after returning from honeymoon, war broke out. Minnie was called back into teaching, as male teachers left for the frontline. Conditions in schools deteriorated, with the NUT complaining of a shortage of resources, LCC cuts resulting in loss of heating, and children anxious about their absent fathers. In 1915, Minnie left her post at Fairclough Street School and became a full-time organiser with the ELFS, a decision urged on by Sylvia Pankhurst. She explained why Minnie was so invaluable:

> I induced [George Lansbury's] son Edgar's wife, née Minnie Glassman, to leave her work as an elementary school teacher and help me as assistant honorary secretary of our federation. She devoted herself mainly to our distress work, and to the League of Rights. She knew the district and people, and in accordance with the first principle of work in our Federation, she was prepared to make herself unreservedly the advocate of the people, and to get the best she could for them. So many would-be uplifters of the poor allow their critical faculties to run amuck, and begin to fancy that after all, 'poor people like that' can manage on very short commons. I always felt I could trust Minnie to realise that under the veneer we humans are all very much alike; and that the most we could get for our poor, was very much less than we all of us need – and a wretched makeshift indeed, for the social equality and assurance we desire. I was more than glad of her aid.[12]

Like the WFL, the ELFS opposed the war, turning their attention to relieving the hardship it caused. They created a clinic to treat hungry and sick children; opened three cost price canteens; set up an employment bureau; established a toy factory, where women could earn a living wage and learn a trade; and established the first Montessori nursery, which Minnie became assistant secretary of.

In February 1915, the ELFS launched The League of Rights for Soldiers' and Sailors' Wives and Relatives. It filled gaps left by the existing non-governmental organisation – the Soldiers' and Sailors' Families Association – which was widely considered inadequate. Minnie became one of The League's leaders.

Servicemen's families paid a penny per month for membership to The League. They acted 'as the family lawyer in the case of well-to-do people, and as the trade union in the case of miners, railwaymen and others.'[13] They supported many families being treated appallingly by the authorities. When the House of Commons revealed that over a third of soldiers invalided out of the army, and half of war widows, received no pension, the League demanded the government pay up. It was outrageous that those who'd answered the call, were treated with such disdain. Legislation eventually passed to create the War Pension Committees, ensuring families got the money they were entitled to.

Across the country nearly 300 committees were established, with 46 in London. Minnie joined the one in Poplar, while continuing her wider work with The League of Rights. Thousands of East Londoners associated Minnie with her work supporting war veterans and their families

Her agitation didn't end there. As the war progressed, patriotism waned, as deprivations caused by the conflict increased. Opponents of the war, like Minnie and Edgar, spoke out more freely. In December 1916, Germany and its allies suggested peace talks. A crowd of 200 peace protestors assembled around the East India Dock Gates in support. Among them were Minnie and Edgar.

Not everyone who gathered was interested in peace. A small group of war supporters arrived, intent on disruption. When they rushed the crowd, the previously passive policemen stepped in to disperse them, with brute force if they had to. They arrested several anti-war protestors, including suffragettes Sylvia Pankhurst, Charlotte Drake and Melvina Walker, along with Edgar and Minnie. In court, they charged Sylvia, Melvina and Charlotte with obstructing the highway, while Melvina incurred an additional charge of using insulting language. They received fines of two pounds each, the equivalent of over £700 today. Edgar and Minnie were released without charge.

This wouldn't be Edgar's only brush with the law. When married men were added to the conscription, Edgar got his papers. The process allowed him the right to claim exemption, which he did on the grounds of being a councillor. His case was heard in September 1917, and the committee was deadlocked. The chairman cast his deciding vote – Edgar was going to war.

Edgar wasn't going to accept being killed in a war he'd so long been opposing. He lodged his appeal, with the following statement:

> The Local Tribunal did not give due consideration to the grounds upon which I based my appeal, but devoted itself to a consideration of irrelevant matter […] I am a member of the Poplar Borough Council and active worker in the Socialist and Political Labour movement of Poplar and East London. This brings me into conflict with my colleagues on the Borough Council. The Tribunal was composed of a majority of my opponents whom I consider to be not the best qualified people to consider my application.[14]

They waited months to hear the outcome, causing the family great strain. Edgar's mother, Bessie, wrote to her friend Mrs Sewell, saying: 'Poor Edgar is appearing again today at Guildhall, I am anxious how he is getting on.'[15] In winter 1918, the news finally came – his exemption was granted.

Meanwhile, Minnie's work with the League of Rights continued. Their home became known as the 'house of hope'. Every morning, men, women and children flocked to their door seeking advice and assistance from the terrible situations they were in.[16] Minnie never turned anyone away. So it's unsurprising that when Minnie stood in what became landmark elections, the people were behind her.

The Labour landslide

East London in the Victorian and Edwardian era is often depicted as a place of misery, with grime and lives barely worth living. Many popular historical accounts were poverty porn –exploiting the condition of the poor in order to generate sympathy and money, by selling newspapers and books, or eliciting charitable donations. These narratives failed to represent the resistance growing since the end of the nineteenth century.

Disillusionment felt by working class people returning from war, who didn't receive a hero's welcome; the 1918 Representation of the People Act, which greatly expanded and diversified the electorate; and a rapidly growing Labour Party, meant society was changing. By the early 1920s, Labour overtook the Liberal Party, becoming the main opposition to the Conservatives.

On this wave of confidence, a number of Labour Party candidates stood in the 1919 local elections in the London Borough of Poplar. Among them was Minnie Lansbury. They swept to power, taking control of the council and marking a radical shift in political representation. For the first time, the councillors looked like the electorate, comprising of dockers, railway workers, labourers and trade unionists.

Amongst the 30 councillors were five women: Nellie Creswell, a laundrette worker and ELFS activist; Jennie Mackay, a trade unionist; Jane Scurr, who'd been on the ELFS delegation to Asquith in 1914; Jane March, a health visitor; and Minnie. In addition, there was Susan Lawrence, who came from a different background. The daughter of a wealthy solicitor, she was a Conservative member of the London County Council between 1910–1912. Then trade unionist, Mary Macarthur, converted her to socialism. Although the men greatly outnumbered the women, in comparison to other borough councils, Poplar was way ahead of its time.

George Lansbury was elected mayor. At the first council meeting, he placed the official insignia around his neck and declared radical change was coming to Poplar. Cheers erupted. After the meeting a triumphant procession made its way around the borough. Celebrations continued for days after, with speeches, dancing and live music in local Labour Party meeting halls.

Then the hard work started. The newly elected councillors drew up a radical programme of social change to tackle the unemployment, hunger and poverty in the borough. They built new housing; implemented a small pox vaccination campaign; set up a dental clinic; and provided free milk and hot meals to the poorest children. By the end of the year, Poplar had one of the lowest infant mortality rates ever. But one burden on Poplar's poorest residents was harder to resolve.

For many years there'd been resistance to the London taxation system, which was seen as grossly unjust to poor boroughs like Poplar. Despite huge levels of poverty in the area, they paid the same rates as richer boroughs. Discontent grew, and the Councillors agreed they wouldn't collect the tax. This didn't go down well with the LCC, who in July 1921 took the matter to the High Court.

When the councillors arrived in court, the gallery of supporters erupted in cheers. They knew they couldn't win as their actions were illegal. So they used their platform to argue the moral case: impossibly high rates in the face of their borough's financial hardship. Predictably, the judge ordered them to pay or face prison, giving them until the end of August.

The Poplar Councillors discussed their options. Would they submit and pay? The women had all been members of the ELFS, and weren't easily intimidated; others were pacifists, who'd faced prison during the war as conscientious objectors. So Cllr Julia Scurr took a deep breath before calmly saying: 'We will just go [to prison]. That is all.'[17]

On the last Wednesday of August, the councillors met for their final meeting. The following day their arrest warrants would be issued, so they needed to put municipal matters in order. After the close of the meeting they sang the socialist anthem, The Red Flag, and made their way to the Town Hall on Poplar High Street. Thousands of supporters greeted them. They read a statement to the crowd:

Thirty of us, members of the Poplar Borough Council, have been committed to prison. This has been done because we have refused to levy a rate on the people of our Borough to meet the demand of the LCC and other central authorities. We have taken this action deliberately, and we shall continue to take the same course until the Government deals properly with the question of unemployment, providing work, or a full maintenance for all, and carries into effect the long-promised and much overdue reform of the equalisation of rates.

Minnie had built up such loyalty with ex-servicemen, the night her arrest warrant came into force they formed a barricade around her house. Five days later the authorities came for her. She thanked her supporters, but insisted on going, to make the point as well as the men that she would stand by her beliefs and stand up for the workers.

A crowd 10,000 strong came out in support of the woman, as they headed to Holloway prison (their male counterparts were sent to Brixton). Minnie was fashionably dressed and appeared relaxed as she walked towards her fate, shaking hands with those who gathered in support. Although Minnie usually shied away from the limelight, she made a speech at Poplar Town Hall before departing, even managing to crack a small joke. An 'appreciative tax payer' presented her with a small bouquet of flowers.[18]

The women climbed in the Sheriff's car, which drove through a crowd of tens of thousands. The women smiled and waved at their supporters, who cheered and sang Jolly Good Fellows. As the car finally disappeared from view, the crowd fell silent. Now it was time for the women to maintain their stand from inside the walls of Holloway Women's Prison.

Inside Holloway

When the women arrived at Holloway they were issued with badges. They refused to wear them. The prison governor knew these were not ordinary inmates, but neither were they the first prisoners of conscience at Holloway. Hundreds of suffragettes had been through its gates, including Sylvia Pankhurst and Adelaide Knight.

As political prisoners, the rebel women councillors were allowed to wear their own clothes, and talk to each other during morning and evening exercise. Jenny Mackay even visited her sick father. However, the conditions in Holloway remained grim. Earlier that summer, the Worker's Dreadnought (formerly the Women's Dreadnought) reported: 'The close confinement is bad for health, and the absolute discipline and lack of contact with the outside world and crush of all initiative makes the struggle for existence on release far, far harder.'

Minnie met the harsh conditions with determination, reportedly even once sliding down the bannister, much to the horror of the warden. Yet while her spirit was strong, her body was not. Shortly after arrival she was transferred to the sick ward. Nellie Creswell was already sent there due to her advanced stage of pregnancy. Despite being unwell herself, Minnie was quick to come to her comrade's aid. When she found out Nellie hadn't been given an opportunity to exercise or access to edible food, she kicked up a fuss. Complaining to the authorities, the women's demands were eventually met.

Meanwhile on the outside, their supporters kept up the fight. On 7th September, 5000 people marched the seven miles from Poplar to Holloway. Sympathisers gave money, distributed leaflets and sent letters to the councillors inside, as well as one of protest to the Home Office. Trade unions kept up vigils outside both Holloway and Brixton prison. In other London boroughs supporters flocked to public meetings demanding their councils take the same action. A vote in Shoreditch and Battersea lost by one count. After a heated debate, Bethnal Green became the first council to come out in solidarity, voting to withhold their taxes.

On 21st September, Nellie Cresswell, who by this point was eight months pregnant, was released on health grounds. She'd initially refused, not wanting to break ranks, but the governor forced her out. On her release she spoke out about the cruelty of the prison system, and urged supporters to keep up the pressure for her comrades.

By now, Stepney was threatening to withhold their taxes too. Fearing an all-out London rebellion, the Government instructed the courts to issue release orders. On 21st October 1921, all the rebel councillors were released. By this time Minnie was so weak she had to be helped into a cab.

Minnie's legacy

In the middle of December 1921, Minnie fell ill with influenza, which within weeks developed into pneumonia. On New Year's Eve she seemed a little better, but the following day she deteriorated again. In the early evening of 1st January 1922, Minnie Lansbury died, aged just 32.

Three days later, a large crowed wearing red flowers and badges gathered outside her home. Tens of thousands more flooded the streets for her funeral procession. Her still loyal ex-servicemen carried the coffin. A week later, at a packed memorial meeting at Bow Baths Hall, Councillor Sam Marsh said: 'No one could say Minnie's stature was large, but all could say her heart was large.'[19] Other Poplar councillors read tributes, and one read a letter from Edgar, who was too grief stricken to attend. The crowd sang the Red Flag, and held collections for the Mayor's Fund to relieve economic distress.

Many other jailed councillors succumbed to early deaths or prolonged ill health, which they attributed to their time in prison. Their sacrifice wasn't for nothing. That same winter Minnie died, Parliament rushed through the Local Authorities (Financial Provisions) Act. It went a significant way to equalising the tax discrepancies between wealthier and poorer boroughs.

Ten years after Minnie's death, a memorial clock was erected at Electric House on Bow Road. It was funded by the public sale of small floral tickets. During WW2, it suffered extensive damage. Again, the public put their hands in their pockets to have it restored. The clock remains today, a poignant reminder of the power of solidarity and the strength of a coal merchant's daughter from one of the poorest corners of the East End.

Chapter 6

Muriel Rise Up!

On the edge of Epping Forest was the hamlet of Leytonstone, part of the parish of Leyton. It had existed since the fourteenth century, and remained a rural, leafy area until the nineteenth century, and the coming of the railways. In 1893, it was home to eight-year-old Muriel Lester, who sat on a train, heading west, watching the trees and grass turn into dust and concrete.

As they reached the East End district of Bow, a foul smell wafted through the windows. It was both sweet and rotten, drifting out of the factories making soap. This perfumed delicacy sold in the finest shops in the West End for a fortune. At its East End source, the steaming of animal bones made the whole neighbour stink.

The train ground to a halt, and Muriel tugged at the window to shut out the smell. Down below she saw a rabbit warren of houses in dilapidated conditions: garden-less; leaking; dirty. She asked her nurse whether people lived down there. The nurse confirmed they did. 'Do they really?' replied Muriel

'They don't feel things the way we way do," said the nurse. 'And even if they did, they've only got themselves to blame. They get drunk. That's why they're poor.'[1]

Muriel and her younger siblings, Kingsley and Dorris, lived in a world of tennis lawns, piano lessons and parties, where the carpets were pulled up so people could dance all night. She was an anxious child however, fearful of the long dark corridors in her grand house; and the heavy tick of the grandfather clock made her heart beat too fast. She became burdened with guilt that perhaps she was idolising her beloved doll, Iris, with her brown curls and big eyes. Was this not blasphemy?[2]

Yet Muriel's parents were not the strict Victorian archetypes. Understanding fear of punishments might encourage lying, Muriel's mother encouraged the children to openly confess their wrongdoings. She promised in return there'd be no anger. Muriel still struggled with confession, storing misdeeds up until the weight of guilt overwhelmed her.

Their religious education was a priority, as Christianity meant everything to her father. Every Sunday, they dressed in clean clothes with starched pinafores. They lined up for inspection, their father checking for polished shoes and neatly combed hair. Before the service, he made each child copy out a text from the Bible. After, they went round with a box to collect pennies for the poor. Yet this stocky man, with his twinkling eyes and Father Christmas whiskers, was easily irritated with church officialdom. He conducted his own Sunday talks, where he challenged the old ideas of punishment and justice, championing the little country churches frequented by working people.

While achieving financial security, Henry Lester, Muriel's father, knew what it was like to go hungry. His grandfather fought in the Napoleonic wars, after being press ganged. He'd been on his way home when an officer seized him. The children were playing in the street, and tried to drag their father away from his captors. Hearing the noise, his wife came out, and pleaded with them to release him. They refused, dragging him away. It was the last the family saw of him for years.

Left without their main income earner, Henry's grandmother tried to find work. But even if successful she could never earn what her husband had. The family had to leave their home and move into a single room, selling everything to buy food.

At only eight years old, Henry's father found work as a bricklayer, becoming the family's main breadwinner. In the bitter cold, and for many long hours, he climbed ladders carrying bricks and mortar on his tiny shoulders. His feet became covered in chilblains, lime working its way through his boots making the infection worse. It was gruelling, painful work, but the little boy kept his family from starvation.

All this time, they had no idea if Henry's grandfather was alive or dead, as there was no reliable postal system at the time. Then one day, a bearded stranger appeared on their doorstep. The younger members of the family stared at this weak, pale man in confusion. But their mother recognised their father at once, and joyfully greeted him.

Henry's father left the building sites, moving into carpentry, finding work with a big firm on the docks. He found religion, which put him in conflict with his father. Their relationship soured, so he left home. He married, and in 1836 Henry was born.

The family income was small, and the Corn Laws kept food prices high and hunger present. Yet they managed to scrape together enough to get Henry an education. At 12 years old, he left school and found work as an apprentice draughtsman in a shipbuilding firm. After completing his apprenticeship, he set up in business with his father.

While the business started well, disaster hit. A fire burnt the firm to the ground. Henry's grandfather had forgotten to pay the insurance premiums, so they lost everything. Dark days followed, and the two men only avoided complete despair because of their faith.

Eventually their luck changed. Hearing of the tragedy, one of the big shipping men agreed to lend Henry the money to start again. Nobody knows what inspired this generosity, but it lifted the family back up again. The business grew into a significant success, known locally for its fair working conditions and pay. Henry went on to become a magistrate, and Chair of the local school board.[3]

School life

Muriel's family left Leytonstone, moving to Loughton in the heart of Epping Forest. Muriel was surrounded by bird song, silver birches and wild roses; honeysuckle sweetened the air; lakes teamed with tadpoles; and clay paths enticed her to adventures in the woods. Yet all this idyl was about to be disrupted.

At a time when it was unusual to educate girls beyond the basics, Muriel was sent away to boarding school in Scotland. It was at her mother's insistence. Her father was opposed, believing it foolish to send children away from a good home. He relented on the advice of the family doctor, who said the Aberdeen air would be good for her constitution. Muriel broadly enjoyed school life, admiring her house-mistress who instilled in all the girls the importance of thinking for themselves. She received a comparatively rounded education for a girl of her time, including literature, European history, Latin and Greek. They were also taught to sew, play the piano, and attended church every Sunday.

She left school at 18, and there'd been talk of Cambridge University. But Muriel wasn't keen on continuing her struggles to reading Greek plays, or translate Latin. Instead, she travelled around Europe, played tennis, received piano and singing lessons, visited school friends, and took charge of a class of boys at Sunday school.

It was during this summer as a lady of leisure that she discovered Tolstoy. This turned her thinking upside down. From an 'absurdly militant young women' she swiftly transitioned into pacifism, because 'once your eyes get opened to [it], you can't shut them again'.[4] Through his writing, she discovered non-violent resistance; and the belief that Christians should be guided by love of one's neighbour and God, rather than Church or state.

Bow life

'Would you like to come to a party in the East End?' a friend said to Muriel one day. 'I'll take you along if you like.'

The last time Muriel had been in Bow she was 12 years old. Prince George, the Duke of York, came to open the new Blackwall Tunnel with his wife. Muriel travelled there by horse and carriage, with her mother and father. She began in high spirits, enjoying the bumpy but pleasant ride. Soon they entered more 'questionable streets'. Houses became shabby, and even a little sinister. The roads filled with people, shouting, waving paper hats and blowing party horns. They had red faces and laughed uncontrollably. While her parents seemed at relative ease, Muriel felt the 'creak and crackle of white silk gloves as I gripped the railing tighter to control my fear.' She didn't dare disclose her discomfort to her parents, who continued to enjoy the show. Yet Muriel waited, tense and wretched, not for the Duke to arrive, but for him to go, so she could leave the awful place.[5]

Many years had passed since; many chats on Sunday afternoon walks with her father; many books by Tolstoy. Curiosity replaced her fear – she'd never come into contact with working class people before, except when they served her on buses, restaurants and in her home. She excepted the invitation and boarded the train with Doris, heading into the heart of the East End.

They walked down narrow, murky streets, lit only by the occasional gas lamp, until they reached the 'factory girls' club'. Inside thin and pale women with bent shoulders, danced and talked. Every minute refreshments were shoved into their hands. Many of the women were the same age as Muriel – nineteen – but seemed far more mature and independent. She reflected on her pampered life, and how they could be so different. While she was expanding her horizons at boarding school, they were chained to a machine for 10–12 hours per day.

The party marked a new era for Muriel. While it was a strain to leave the beauty of Epping Forest, stepping into tar and concrete, with the fumes from the factories and breweries, the people lifted her mood. Soon she visited weekly, dedicated to finding out more. She wanted to know their thoughts and feelings. She longed to be invited into one of their homes. Eventually her wish was granted. An elderly woman who lived near the club, offered her a cup of cocoa before setting off home. She eagerly accepted.

The house was fairly typical working-class accommodation. Heat came from a small open fire. There was a dresser, with row upon row of cups and saucers, and china ornaments on a mantlepiece. The rooms were small, with people jostling for spare seats. The only time they all sat down at once was for the sacred Sunday lunch. The kitchen sink performed various functions, from washing dishes to shaving faces. Above it was a row of nails, off which hung toothbrushes, flannels, towels and an unframed mirror.

While Muriel was thrilled to get this glimpse into East End living, she didn't romanticise working class life. While in Bow, she came up against suicide for the first time, which was often driven by debt. Loan sharks lent families money when in a crisis, charging huge interest rates. The deals were often done at a pub, over too many drinks. When unable to keep up with the weekly payments, the borrower took another loan. Many debts were due to medical costs, so the 1911 National Insurance Act reduced these exploitative schemes.

Outside of Bow, Muriel continued to live in a parallel world of balls, picnics and long days at the races. It was at a tennis party these two worlds collided. The Bow women told Muriel that a factory owner was cutting pay, but they were scared of speaking out for fear of losing their jobs. When Muriel heard a woman at the party expel the virtues of this same factory owner, she had to speak out.

A few weeks later, the woman from the party stopped her in the street. She'd spoken to the factory owner, passing on what Muriel had said about the girls' wages. Muriel was horrified – had she got the Bow women in trouble? Might they even lose their jobs? When the next club night came, she offered her sincere apologies, yet discovered there was no need. The matter was investigated, and the women received a healthy amount of back pay. This unique position Muriel found herself in – living between two different worlds – shaped much of her future activism.[6]

From these shaky beginnings, Muriel's confidence grew. After a year or two of visiting Bow, a new church minister invited her to lead the women's meeting. Her initial reaction was to refuse, overwhelmed by the idea. Yet Doris urged her on, offering support.

At their first meeting a group of 30 turned up, cajoled into attending with the promise of tea. Yet something stuck. The women continued to meet weekly, and months grew into years. They invited speakers on workers' rights; held talks from returning travellers; gave health advice; and campaigned on women's suffrage. Muriel's faith remained central to her work, the group praying and reading the bible together each meeting.

Through this group, Muriel realised that wives and home-makers were some of 'the most sensible, experienced and well-balanced people in the borough'.[7] Yet she also recognised them as exploited, unpaid, and lacking representation. So she called a mass meeting, and form a committee to carry out whatever support was needed. They chose a system of home helps – a group of middle-aged women paid to support other families when needed. This might be when a child fell ill; to cook dinner if the mother was unwell; clean the house or do the laundry in event of emergency; or mind the children.

Muriel was not the only women in East London recognising both the importance and the strain these women were under. Alice Model founded the Sick Room Help Society in 1895, which despatched maternity nurses to the homes of sick, poor and confined women. In 1911, this evolved into the Jewish Maternity Hospital in Whitechapel.[8] In the 1918 Report of the Medical Officer of Health for Leyton, a special mention is given to the Leyton Health Society in supporting 'the council's efforts to save infant life'. They sent volunteers into homes to support mothers with 'feeding and clothing children, and the hygiene of the home.'[9] Yet it would take until 1973 before Home-Start formed, a nationwide network of home helps. These East London women were the pioneers of today's welfare state, proving that radical change often comes from the bottom up.

Kingsley Hall

It was Doris who took up temporary residence in Bow first, sleeping at the home of a women's meeting member. She became devoted, declaring her wish to permanently settle in the area. She persuaded Muriel to take an attic room with her at Doric Lodge, a severe looking extension to the missionary training college. The accommodation was noisy, and out near Mile End, far from where they wanted to be. So they moved to a couple of rooms in a house near the Bryant & May factory. Although better located, it was filthy. While saying her prayers one evening, a rat scuttled across the floor in front of Muriel. She called to mind all the hermits and saints throughout history to calm herself.[10]

In 1912, Kingsley got interested in Bow, leaving behind his business interests. The three siblings took on a small house at 60 Bruce Road, which was in the middle of a long terrace. There was a church at one end and a doctor at the other, with a pub somewhere in the middle. Like the other houses, it was in poor condition, with battered iron railings and a broken gate; the varnish had worn off the front door years ago, blistering and peeling, and the knocker was too rusted to move; inside the walls were damp, and there were mice. But they deloused, scrubbed, cleaned and repapered. The little workers' house became a focal point of socialist activity. George Lansbury and family visited for tea; a Poplar councillor came to discuss opening an adult education centre; another arrived with his wife to educate them on local politics. They debated infant mortality rates, slum clearance and poor relief.

On Sundays they squeezed twelve people into one of the tiny rooms for lunch. In the warmer summer months, they brought chairs out to the front to sit and talk with their neighbours. Boys played cricket in the street, and girls skipped rope. The younger ones pretended to be mummies and daddies, adopting firm voices while lugging around chubby baby brothers and sisters. Older adolescents played cards.[11]

The question of how to reach the masses was frequently batted around by leading thinkers of the day, especially within the church. Nobody thought of going to live with them. Muriel, Doris and Kingsley realised it was the quickest way to build solidarity, as they struggled with the same landlord, shared tips on delousing and how to stop a leaking roof.

Yet Kingsley's stay in Bow was a short one. In autumn 1913, his appendix trouble started up again, more seriously this time. He returned home to be nursed, and went to the Italian Riviera to convalesce.

Meanwhile in Bow, conversations continued around fighting the oppressions of capitalism. Muriel and Doris attended meetings; listened to speeches in Victoria Park; and talked late into the night about how to improve life in the East End. While Muriel found answers in her faith, many locals didn't share her passion. So she set them a challenge: they should attend a ten-week Bible study group; if they couldn't find answers within these teachings she agreed to start a campaign to shut down all the neighbourhood churches. The locals couldn't resist.

So on a Sunday in May 1914, a group of seven began work. They sang hymns, read prayers, shared life experiences and eventually came to a decision. One of Bow's biggest issues was the lack of social spaces

– the only place where people could spend leisure time was in the pub. No wonder alcoholism plighted so many working-class lives. The group bounced around the idea of creating a teetotal pub – a type of communal living room where people could meet friends. It would be run by locals for locals 'without profit or propaganda.'[12]

Yet these dreams were interrupted. On 4th August 1914, Germany declared war on Britain. Muriel took the news to Kingsley, finding him in bed again. He rose only to go to the hospital, where one operation followed another. Six weeks later he was back home, his time on earth moving towards its end. Muriel sat on his bed, holding his hand, soothing him with gentle conversation. Then he said: 'Muriel, it's getting dark.' His breathing slowed, his hand grew cold, and he slipped away.[13]

As the war marched on, Muriel was glad that Kingsley was neither glorified for killing nor ostracised for refusing. Instead, the family found a more fitting memorial. Using the little money Kingsley left in his will, and a loan from their father, they started work on the teetotal public house. They purchased a small chapel on Eagling Road, and in 1915 Kingsley Hall opened: a people's house, where friends and neighbours could meet for 'social, educational and recreational intercourse without barriers of class, colour or creed.'[14]

On the opening night of Kingsley Hall, Muriel threaded her way through the poorly lit streets. As she approached the party, a darkness rose up inside her so abruptly she had to stop. The grief she'd put on hold to build Kingsley Hall overtook her. In the middle of the dark street she wept for the loss of her dear brother.

This darkness lingered for many weeks. Her heart raced 'like an engine' and she felt like she was falling down a 'steep and narrow well'. Doctors came and prescribed a period of rest, which lasted eight months.[15]

Her recovery was long, and she often felt frustrated. Even after returning to work, she had to take long breaks. She'd lock herself in a room, lie on the floor and focus on her breathing. Her work in Bow, and the death of Kingsley, had pushed her to breaking point. Finally, she realised that 'work is not an end in itself. It is one's way of doing it that counts, one's way of life.'[16]

War

As conflict driven hunger gripped the East End, Kingsley Hall set up a dinner club to feed people. In 1916, air raids began. A group calling themselves the Kingsley Watch Patrol used a room in the hall, staying up talking and smoking all night. If news came by telephone of an imminent raid, they took to the streets to alert the neighbours.

Muriel wouldn't pray for victory. Instead, she went to the docks to preach on the senselessness of war. When conscription began, a number of her friends refused to join up. She accompanied them to tribunals, and visited in prison. She looked in on the wives and families, arranging collections if they were in financial difficulty.

The armistice celebrations in 1918 were short-lived for Muriel, as news came of hunger across Europe. At Kingsley Hall, they called on newspaper editors to tell the truth, and lobbied parliament. Dissatisfied with the rate of progress, they turned themselves into 'living newspapers', walking from the East End to the House of Commons. They demanded the Government send milk to starving children in Europe.'[17] Kingsley Hall members adopted an Austrian child called Marie, paying for her to stay with a local family for over two years.

Muriel kept up her public speaking. In each speech she drew attention to the violence committed in the name of victory. In the occupied Rhineland area, French troops were raping and sexual assaulting women in local villages. She said: '… to turn victory into violence against women, a physical and psychological mastery, and to call it peace, is to begin a process that must destroy human joy.'[18]

After Minnie

Having made a name for herself locally, Muriel was nominated to replace Minnie Lansbury on Poplar Council. These were big boots to fill, and Muriel feared she didn't have Minnie's knowledge or devotion. She turned the role down. Instead, she took over running the Maternity and Child Welfare Committee, which had been in Minnie's remit. She set up a new dental clinic for mothers, improved the health of babies with artificial sunlight treatment, and distributed free milk to the poorest families.

These interventions came at a cost. The government told them to cut down on their expenditure. Muriel and her committee argued it was against their conscience to reduce the milk supply, and refused the Governmental order. She was called to Whitehall to face questions from the Ministry of Health.

Muriel refused to back down. When asked why she refused to comply, when every other local authority had agreed, she replied: 'Ours is the only Maternity and Child Welfare Committee composed wholly of people who live down the same streets and alleys as the children. We see them every day. We should have to watch them growing pale and thin and weak if the milk grant was to be lowered.'[19] Three weeks later they won their battle, and the grant was maintained.

The Children's House

Muriel and Doris were both deeply committed to the welfare of children. But it was Doris who trained as a teacher, and the driving force behind the Children's House. Originally they established a nursery at Kingsley Hall, for 26 boys and girls aged between two and four years old. There were toys to play with, and books to borrow if they had none at home. They taught them about Greek myths, and put on performances. Excursions were run to Epping Forest to explore nature, and have a break from the city's dirt and squalor. A doctor came every Friday for medical check-ups, and the children received 'sunlight treatment' to prevent rickets.[20]

Yet the sisters had a slogan: 'The best is not too good for the children of Poplar'.[21] They knew Kingsley Hall wasn't suitable, due to its lack of a south window, which meant little light came into the nursery. More importantly, there was no outdoor space. The children needed an open-air school, or at least a garden. A new mission began.

They asked for help from the more affluent residents in West Bow, including two ex-mayors, a Liberal and a socialist. Nobody was forthcoming. In the end they took the children to their own small back garden at 60 Bruce Road. They loved it, but the neighbours didn't. Muriel and Doris also knew it would never pass a school inspection.

Eventually their father offered to put up some money so they could build a new nursery. A row of four dilapidated houses stood at the far end of Kingsley Road, owned by the London County Council. Muriel convinced them to sell the site, and in September 1923, London's first Children's House was born. Once again using her personal contacts, it was officially opened by H.G Wells.

The building had a fat roof, which they turned into a playground. It also provided a space for the children to sleep on, in both the summer and winter. There were assembly halls, and a kitchen and dining room. The created a graded education programme, using the Montessori technique; set up a parents' association; and organised holidays and summer camps. Artist, illustrator and writer, Eve Garnett, created a twelve-metre mural inside the Children's House. Although in dilapidated condition, it still exists, depicting a line of children walking through an East End street, towards a door that opens into a magical, green forest. A second Children's House opened in Dagenham, Essex, in 1932. It was the first purpose-built nursery in the area.

Strike!

In 1926, Muriel rose into action again, this time in solidarity with the miners. They'd been at loggerheads with their employers for years, over reduced pay for more hours. Now they had to work an extra hour every day, while losing an hours pay. Their slogan was: not an hour on the day, not a penny off the pay. But on 1st May 1926, around a million miners refusing to accept the new working conditions, were 'locked out' of pits and their wages stopped. And so the strike began.

When the TUC declared their support for the miners' strike, other industrial workers walked out, including road transport, rail, docks, printers, electricity and gas, and iron and steel. Britain's first general strike had begun. In Bow, George Lansbury told the people to fold their arms and do nothing. They amused themselves with concerts, singing and other entertainment. In Victoria Park, soldiers gathered in case the government declared marshal law.

The main goal of the strike was to force the government to reopen negotiations by controlling the movement of supplies, particularly food. To Britain's leaders, this mass industrial action looked worrying like the Communist Revolution in Russia, less than a decade before. Although revolution was far from the workers' minds, the government whipped up a fear of anarchy, persuading all sorts of people to break the strike. Volunteers came forward to drive buses and trains, or work on the docks. The country was split, with the dispute described as 'the cloth cap versus the debutant set.'[22] An infamous group from Cambridge University called themselves the Trinity 50, because they met under the clock at Trinity College. Their chauffeurs drove them down to the docks in their Bentleys, where they helped unload cargo.

After nine days, a third of the TUC's income was gone. Holding out much longer risked bankruptcy. So they entered negotiations with the mine owners. But the deal they struck still included wage cuts and pit closures. The Miners' Federation turned it down. On the tenth day, Muriel and her friends from Kingsley Hall gathered around the radio to hear the latest news. The TUC had crumbled. Prime Minister, Stanley Baldwin declared the strike over.

It wasn't over for Muriel, however. They'd made thousands of tiny miners lamps, which were sold to strike sympathisers for a shilling. Muriel took a pile up to Victoria Park. Turning herself once again into a human newspaper, she rose awareness about the suffering of the miners, encouraging people to buy the lamps. She raised over £10, equivalent to more than £500 today. She donated the money to the miners' unions.

While recovering from the General Strike defeat, news filtered through about a man in India called Gandhi. Muriel devoured copies of his newspaper, Young India. Her life was about to take a whole new turn.

Gandhi and the people of Bow

While Muriel often travelled within Europe, during the 1930s her horizons expanded. She developed an internationalist perspective, believing that humans should unite across national, political, cultural, racial and class divides; that they should cooperate in order to ease suffering and bring about peace. This political journey began in India.

One evening, a friend of Muriel's brought Professor Gangulee to speak at Kingsley Hall. Gangulee was the son-in-law of Rabindranath Tangore, most famous as a Bengali writer and first non-European to win the Nobel Prize for Literature. Muriel and Professor Gangulee struck up an immediate friendship. Walking together to the tube station one day, he said to her: 'I wish you would go to India and see things for yourself. If you could spare time to stay […] a month with Mr Gandhi, and a month looking around, I would arrange everything for you.'[23]

That was how Muriel found herself in India, standing in silence with Gandhi in his cell-like room. He worked at a spinning wheel, and asked her to sit by him. Still in the habit of letting the thoughts burst out of her, she said: 'Mr Gandhi, will you please come to England, I think it is important that you should.'

Gandhi was reluctant, saying his mission was resisting the British in India. He didn't have time to teach her people anything.

'But Gandhi,' Muriel replied. 'I don't want you to come to England in order to teach us. I want you to come and learn from us.'[24]

While Muriel couldn't convince Gandhi that time, five years later, in 1931, he eventually came to London. It was for the Round Table Conference, to debate independence for India. Muriel knew the bare walls and stone floored accommodation at Kingsley Hall would suit him perfectly. She wrote a carefully worded letter, using her contacts to get it to him. While there'd been plenty of good offers, including by King George for accommodation in the West End, and newly redecorated apartments in Hampstead, Muriel was right. In his reply, Gandhi wrote: 'Of course I would rather stay at Kingsley Hall than anywhere else in London, because there I shall be among the same sort of people as those to whom I have devoted my life.'[25]

The authorities complained about the plan, but Muriel and Gandhi's stubbornness and determination won. Five rooms were cleared out, so they were suitably bare for his party. On his arrival, the people of Bow massed in Kingsley Hall, spilling into the street. Gandhi climbed the stairs to the veranda, and waved to the crowds below.

The people of Bow showed Gandhi the East End spirit, inviting him to their social event, which took place at Kingsley Hall every Saturday evening. Everyone came: young and old; mothers and fathers; even the children. There were games, dancing, and refreshments. Gandhi moved through the hall, shaking people's hands and cuddling babies. Eventually he rested by the piano. When the music struck up, one of the mothers approached him, and said: 'Mr Gandhi, come and have a dance with me.' With a look of surprise and pleasure at being treated with so little formality, he replied: 'But I'm afraid I don't know how to dance. Will you see that I learn please, Muriel?'[26]

Gandhi stayed at Kingsley Hall for nearly three months. During that time he travelled around the country, visiting everyone from cotton workers in Lancashire, to attending the King's garden party at Buckingham Palace. Yet he made time for the people of Bow. Every morning he'd take a walk. Learning his regular routine, people waited on corners to accompany him. Others got up early to wish him good morning when he walked past their house. On hearing it was Gandhi's birthday, the children in Doris' nursery made him gifts. At the Children's House, he carefully took their presents – a small selection of toys – promising to pass them on to the children of his Ashram school in India.

While no mention is made in Muriel's autobiography, Gandhi's sexual exploitation of girls and young women in his Ashram is well documented. It's not clear if she knew. Gandhi had revealed his 'experiments with chastity' in his weekly newspaper.[27] Muriel mentions frequently that she read this paper from cover to cover. Did she somehow miss it or gloss over it? Either way, we must now come to terms with the complexity of so-called heroes. For the sake of the victims, we must not erase the difficult parts of Gandhi's story.

Internationalism and WW2

The inter-war years saw Muriel embark on a series of trips to Japan, China and a number more times to India. Through this travel she deepened her understanding of the impacts of imperialism and colonialism, once again by living among the people. During this time, she also embarked on a speaking tour of the US, which raised vital funds when Kingsley Hall hit financial hardship.

Back in Bow, things were changing. A programme of slum clearance began, tearing down dilapidated old houses, but along with them, rabbit hutches, fowl houses and small patches of garden. In their place they built flats, piled on tops of each other. While they had better amenities, it broke up the streets where families had chatted and children played. There were playgrounds for the younger children, but nowhere for the older ones. Mothers worried about where they would go, and if they were getting in trouble with the law. Muriel said: '… we were congratulated by press, parliament and foreign visitors alike. But a major operation had been performed on the personality of the tenants from which many of them never recovered.'[28]

Muriel packed her bags once more, heading this time for Europe. On her return in 1938, everyone was talking about Hitler. War felt close in Bow that summer, with the measuring and fitting of gas masks. While the families waited in queues, Muriel distracted the children, dragging their stares away from the horrifying sight of a baby in a gas mask. While people across Britain continued to hope that Hitler could be stopped, in the East End war felt inevitable. A grim atmosphere spread across Bow during the summer of 1939.

When Britain finally declared war on Germany, Muriel was on the Queen Mary, sailing towards the USA. She was uncertain what to do: return home or continue on her mission? While she hated to be apart from her country and its people, she felt unsure of what to say if she was with them. She loathed Hitlerism, but remained committed to pacifism. She'd seen moments over the past decade when Britain and its allies could've stopped Hitler, and failed. It felt irrational to now try and solve these problems by killing each other. Once again, Muriel turned to her faith to find answers. Each morning she joined with other Christian pacifists in silent worship, waiting for guidance from God.

On arrival in New York, she regained her confidence. She wrote to Lord Lothian at the British Embassy saying she wouldn't support the war. She joined a team assembled by the Federation Council of Churches, arranging a speaking tour of universities around the country. By 1940, stories emerged of children in Europe facing starvation. Her church group advocated dropping one meal a week in order to raise funds for a children's refugee camp in Free France. They produced leaflets to encourage others to join the movement, and lobbied the British government to send over food ships. Back in Britain, Churchill did not like this bothersome woman meddling in his affairs. Muriel received warnings from her friends to be careful.

In Bow, the phoney war was over. Between September 1940 and May 1941, London experienced an unprecedented attack from Nazi Germany. During the Blitz, it's estimated that 12,000 metric tons of bombs were dropped on London, killing nearly 30,000 civilians.[29] As a hub for imports and war goods, the East End was a prime bombing target. In Bethnal Green alone, 80 tons of bombs fell, affecting 21,700 houses, killing 555 people, and seriously injuring 400 more.[30] For Tower Hamlets as a whole, a total of 2,221 civilians were killed, and 7,472 injured, with 46,482 houses destroyed.[31]

The Government was accused of failing to provide adequate shelters to protect civilians in East London. The proscribed trench shelters filled with water, street level shelters got destroyed, and the DIY Anderson shelters only offered limited protection. Many went to tube shelters, where they endured long, sleepless nights, packed in with hundreds of other scared people.

Doris wrote to Muriel when bombs hit their doorstep:

Gunfire and shelling kept increasing in volume till there came a terrific blast. We felt it must be the last trump. All the lights went out and Kingsley Hall quivered. There was a crash of shattering glass, followed by a tremendous roar of falling buildings. Then sudden quiet, broken by the clamour of fire and ambulance bells. When the All Clear sounded at last we staggered out in early dawn to find houses down all around us. It seemed impossible that we had escaped, but we had.[32]

Kingsley Hall hadn't completely escaped the terror. While the building remained standing, most of the windows were blown out, and the heavy oak doors blasted off their hinges. It was sheer luck it was not worse – the factory opposite was reduced to rubble.

Waterless, gas-less and lightless, the people of Bow came together to clean up. Black with smoke and smothered in dust, they worked. Washing became a privileged they only dreamed of, remaining in the same clothes for days on end. As they swept up broken glass, and cleared soot from windows, someone switched on an urn and passed around gratefully received cups of cocoa.

There was a constant exodus of women and children from the East End, either bombed or evacuated out. Yet as stories filtered back of abuse and neglect in some of the evacuation schemes, mothers faced an impossible decision: keep their children with them; or send them into the hands of complete strangers? Doris hatched a plan. She wrote to her landowning friends, asking if they could find space for the children; to create a kind of East End boarding school in the country. The Duke of Bedford offered her a property. Within 24 hours a group of excited children assembled outside Kingsley Hall, with suitcases, packed lunches and gas masks. Neighbours rushed around trying to find transport. Finally, they found 'a chap who could do it for five quid.' The engine was warming up when the siren began to wail. Should they chance it and go, or wait and risk losing the transport? The mothers urged them to leave. Doris and the children piled inside the van with their suitcases. They waved them off with loud and tearful cheers. As they rounded the corner, the All Clear sounded.

The house had been untenanted for years, so they set to work scrubbing, sorting and unpacking. They prepared hot food and drinks for the children, and the Red Cross arrived with blankets. There were no beds, so they stuffed sacks with straw, donated by a local farmer. The children explored the grounds, delighted to find trees, a mill-pond, a stream with a tiny island and waterfalls. They'd been transported out of their war zone into an entirely new world.[33]

Back in the US, Muriel received word from an American missionary in Uruguay, who said the country was overrun with visitors. They were pressing the Latin American world to support the Allies, claiming it was their Christian duty to fight. They urgently needed a strong pacifist voice – could Muriel help? It seemed far away and she remained worried about Doris and her friends in Bow. Yet she never turned down a challenge, so agreed.

The journey hit obstacles from the start. There were delays with passports, visas blocked, and even rumours she was pro- Nazi. Eventually she made it to Peru, where she talked with young people, and preached in city churches. She sailed south. On reaching Chile, she received news that her good friend, and treasurer of Kingsley Hall, was killed in the Blitz. Onwards to Argentina, to meet Jewish refugees. One told of their escape from Hitler's concentration camps. Finally, to Uruguay, where she spent eleven days giving radio broadcasts, speaking at the university, and visiting a prayer school.

Finally, it was time to return to the US, but passport trouble held her up in Buenos Aires. She was refused permission to re-enter, unless she promised not to lecture or give any more press interviews. She said she couldn't make such a promise. They persisted, but so did Muriel. Eventually she was cleared to leave, the officials saying they were assured she would keep her promise, even though she'd never made one.

She boarded a ship to embark on twelve days of travel back to New York. But on reaching Trinidad, two policeman approached Muriel and told her to collect her things from her cabin. She asked if she was being arrested, and they said she wasn't.

'Then suppose I say I won't come, what happens?' she replied.

'Er-in that case-er-I'm afraid-er-we would have to find means to induce you to do so.'[34]

Muriel negotiated some time for dinner, and then let the policemen escort her from the ship. They took her to a hotel, and told her not to leave the grounds. The following day an officer informed her that she was under detention, and would be transported to an internment camp.

A young commandant greeted Muriel on her arrival. Despite the armed guards and barbed wire, he welcomed her as if at a holiday home. He sang the praises of the camp leader, stating the facilities were the second best in the Empire. After searching her bags, Muriel was directed to her quarters.

Her room contained a canvas stretcher bed, a chair, a shelf, enamel mug, plate, cup, saucer, knife, fork and a spoon. There were two pillow cases, two towels, and a not very clean blanket. The bathrooms were small but tidy, with a couple of cold-water sinks, and a toilet. An old tin pierced with holes hung from the ceiling, which passed as a shower.

The following morning, she met some of her fellow internees, who were a mix of Germans and Italians; a Polish stoker taken off a torpedoed ship; a colonial woman journalist; and a four-year-old boy, who trotted around with a clockwork engine. The largest community were the Jews, who lived in a different part of the camp, separated by barbed wire.

Muriel struck up a friendship with an Irish woman called Frank, who was a teacher in a convent school in Trinidad. Along with another Irish woman, they noticed the poor conditions of the local workers, and began agitating for them. Eventually their school told them to choose between teaching and activism. The chose the latter.

The women published a monthly magazine called New Dawn, gaining a thousand subscribers. They organised with trade unions, and held open-air meetings all over the island. Their work was not appreciated by the local authorities, who detained them. They were threatened with deportation, before internment at the camp. The pressure got too much for Frank's friend, who killed herself a few months after their arrival.

Life in the camp passed slowly for Muriel. Most people staked out some territory, and she claimed hers under a tree near the women's toilets. Here was a space where she could pray, read, write her journal, play her pipe, and sleep. She prepared meals with Frank on a small stove, laying their corner of the table with a small coloured tablecloth. Pooling their money together they were able to put together a decent menu.

In the evenings, they read plays and formed a small drama group, although only Shakespeare was available in sufficient numbers. Later in the night, the trees illuminated as tiny, silver fireflies dance amongst the branches, nature providing the internees with a spectacular light show.

After 50 days in the camp, Muriel was called to the office and told a government official was on his way to see her. A highly polish car pulled up, and out stepped a tall Englishman, who shook Muriel's hand. In his other he held her passport. He announced she would be going home – clearly someone had been lobbying for her.

This didn't move things forward as smoothly as Muriel hoped. Officials knew that an ex-alderman of the socialist borough of Poplar, might be a nuisance if let free amongst the working people and trade unions. So after 12 days sailing, they reached Scotland and she once again found herself under detention. She was repeatedly interviewed before being taken to a police station in Glasgow.

Muriel was escorted by a policewoman, who was small, elderly, with 'fizzy hair and bent shoulders'. She looked like she'd stepped out of the pages of a Dickens' novel.[35] Muriel was taken to her cell and given a mattress and blanket, which smelt of stale urine. Inside were two chairs, a little table and an un-flushed toilet built into the corner. There was a sink too, but it was broken, producing no water.

Around 11pm, the prison erupted into screams and shouts, as the city's drunk and disorderly filtered in. Some shook the metal doors, while others broke down sobbing. In the early hours of the morning, Muriel eventually fell asleep. An hour later she was woken for an inspection. Around 6pm the following evening, Muriel's belongings were returned to her. She was being transported to London. Like the suffragettes and Poplar rebel women, Muriel was heading to Holloway.

Muriel had been to Holloway before, but as a guest lecturer. This time she was marched up a stone staircase, and told to undress. She was weighed, queried about her age and health, and if she'd had a sexually transmitted infection. Then she was searched for lice.

She was taken to the third floor, which was reserved for internees. As a political prisoner, Muriel was allowed to wear her own clothes and not made to do any work. Yet the accommodation was harsh, with little more than a bed made out of a box in a tiny cell. The food was stodgy and starchy. They were woken each morning with the turn of a well-oiled key, and the announcement it was half past six.

Muriel's most pressing issue was getting a telegram to Doris, which took several requests to secure. The next day, the wardress ushered her down a set of passages and staircases. She expected a visitor, probably a Quaker. Instead, her beloved Doris sat in the waiting room. Muriel wondered if they were allowed to hug, before deciding nobody was going to stop her.

Following the visit, Doris phoned 'a person of influence', who answered with surprise: 'What? Muriel in Holloway? We must get her out.' Two days later she was finally on her way home.[36]

Post war

In 1950, Muriel and Doris moved back to Loughton, naming the small home they shared Kingsley Cottage. Muriel continued to take an interest in the East End and peace movements, while caring for Doris, who'd developed dementia. Muriel was 75 before she felt ready to retire from full time work. Five years later she was made Freeman of the Borough of Poplar, in recognition of the huge contribution she'd made to the community. Doris died in 1965, and Muriel three years later. Kingsley Hall held a service, and on 4th April her body was donated to science. At the time of her death she was renowned worldwide, including in Japan, where she was dubbed 'the mother of world peace.'[37] It's believed she may have been nominated for the Nobel Peace Prize, although records weren't kept prior to 1939.[38]

Muriel's legacy

Muriel was a vivacious campaigner, who touched the lives of many in East London. Sometimes in small ways, such as entertaining children in a queue for gas masks; other times it was momentous, such as preaching pacifism across South America.

Reading about her life can leave you feeling a little breathless. Yet what we could interpret as a period of burn out, Muriel processed with impressive clarity for the time. Generations before Audre Lorde defined self-care as a political act, Muriel Lester was cultivating similar ideas. Using mindfulness and re-evaluating what is now called work/life balance, she continued the fight well into her twilight years.

While this is essentially a story about Muriel, she can't be separated from her sister, Doris. Together they made an indomitable pair. Alice Mackay, the project coordinator for the Muriel Lester archives, explains how the sisters' personalities interacted: 'Muriel was spiritual and yet very determined. People always say that Doris was the one who was much more friendly and jolly [...] reading between the lines, [Muriel] was a little scarier [...] she had very strong ideas about how things should be done.'[39]

Yet Muriel was an inspiration to many, including young people. Sylvia Bishop was born in 1925, and attended the Children's Home. She has fond recollections: 'My best memories are when Muriel came to talk, when she'd come back from India and she'd tell us about her life and what she'd done and so forth and I remember being absolutely sort of transfixed with hero worship and whatnot and my devotion to India started right there.'[40]

Following the formation of the welfare state in 1945, the government took on much of the community work of Kingsley Hall. It remained open however, as a youth hostel and community activity centre. In 1965, the Scottish psychiatrist, R D Laing, asked to use the hall for himself and a group of patients with mental disorders. Laing was part of the anti-psychiatry movement, which formed during the 1960s, and lasted until around 1975. It was a collective of radical thinking psychiatrists, who rejected the medical model of mental illness. Laing argued that conditions like schizophrenia were a 'rational response to an insane world'. They challenged the reliability of psychiatric diagnosis; questioned the effectiveness of psychiatric medications; and raised concerns about equal human rights and freedoms. With the Kingsley Hall experiment, Laing turned the world of psychiatry on its head. He created a community where there were no locks on doors, no anti-psychotic drugs administered, and patients were allowed to come and go as they pleased. There were all-night therapy sessions, role-reversals, and marathon Friday night dinners hosted by Laing and visited by mystics, academics and celebrities, including, Sean Connery. The experiment ended in 1970, when two patients jumped off the roof.[41]

While many of these techniques would be considered both unethical and extremely dangerous today, like Muriel, Laing was a revolutionary thinker. He challenged the authority of the medical establishment, family and gender roles, breaking stigma around mental health.

For the next decade, Kingsley Hall was boarded up, falling into disrepair. It was re-awoken in 1980, when it was used on the set of the film Gandhi, directed by Richard Attenborough. Along with the Kingsley Hall Action Group, the director raised enough funds to carry out an extensive refurbishing. Many of the local community contributed their skills and commitment to bring Kingsley Hall back into life, as a usable community centre.

In 1985, Kingsley Hall reopened, running activities including youth groups, holiday outings, workshops, advice surgeries, wedding functions and educational projects. Along with the Children's Home, Kingsley Hall remains open today for the community, and to preserve the memory of these amazing sisters of East London.[42]

Women in a match factory.

The match women.

Sarah Dearman (nee Chapman).
(*Thanks to Sarah Chapan's family*)

Sarah with her husband Charles Dearman.
(*Thanks to Sarah Chapman's family*)

Sarah and her grandson Frederick Dearman.
(*Thanks to Sarah Chapman's family*)

Jewish immigrants arrive at Tilbury docks.

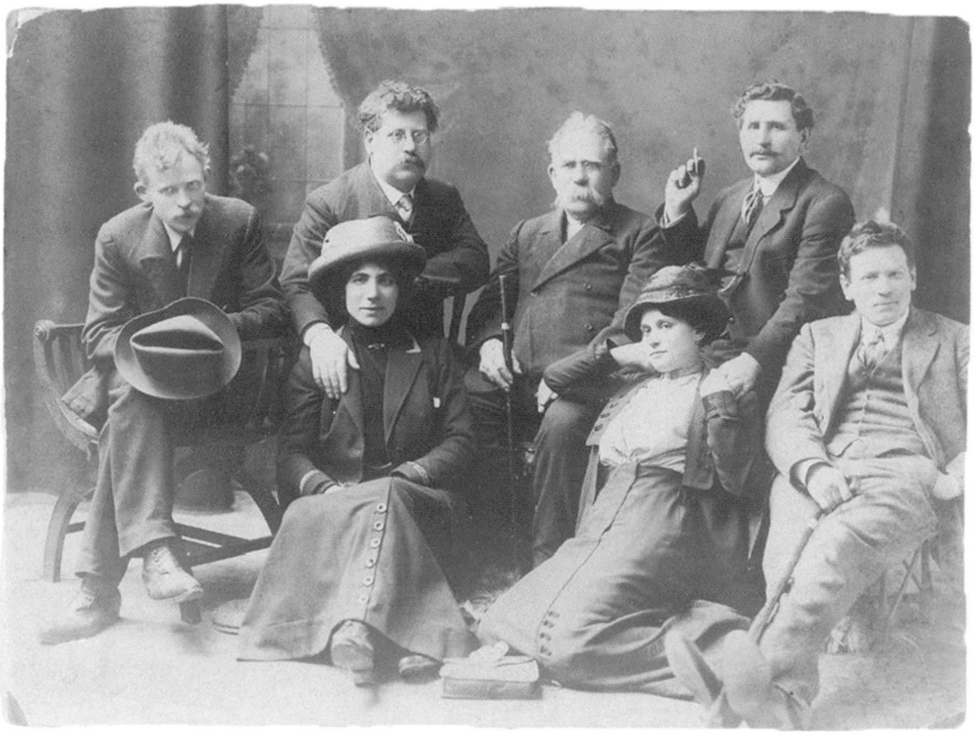

Milly Witkop (front left) with Rudolph Rocker (behind).

The Daily Mirror

THE MORNING JOURNAL WITH THE SECOND LARGEST NET SALE.

No. 1,057. Registered at the G. P. O. as a Newspaper. THURSDAY, MARCH 21, 1907. One Halfpenny.

SUFFRAGETTES STORM THE HOUSE—DESPERATE ENCOUNTER WITH THE POLICE—WHOLESALE ARRESTS.

The suffragettes made a most determined onslaught on the House of Commons yesterday afternoon, and many arrests were made, as all efforts to persuade the demonstrators to go away quietly failed. (1) Shows one of the attacking party struggling in the grasp of two burly constables. (2) Lady Harberton (a prominent suffragette) entering the House to see the Prime Minister. (3) and (4) Two more demonstrators being quietly but firmly led away by the "men in blue."—(Daily Mirror and Half-Tones.)

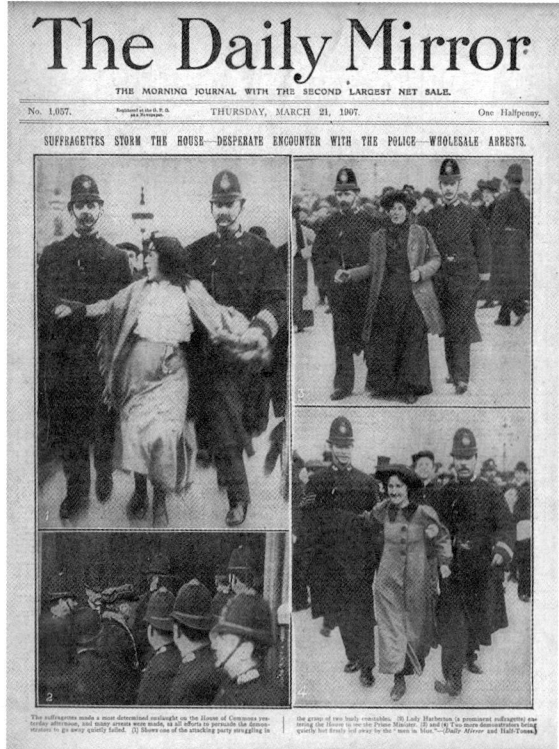

Suffragettes on the front page of the Daily Mirror 1907.

Suffragettes daily exercise at Holloway Prison.

Eva Slawson. (*Share Uk illustration by Laura Greenan*)

Minnie with husband Edgar Lansbury.
(*Family photograph, courtesy of Selina Gellert, great niece of Minnie Lansbury*)

Muriel and her father Henry Lester. (*Muriel Lester Collection of the Kingsley Halls' Heritage Committee*)

Muriel and Doris Lester. (*Muriel Lester Collection of the Kingsley Halls' Heritage Committee*)

Kingsley Lester. (*Muriel Lester Collection of the Kingsley Halls' Heritage Committee*)

Kingsley Hall today. (*Gordon Joly*)

The Children's House. (*Muriel Lester Collection of the Kingsley Halls' Heritage Committee*)

Children in the East End during The Blitz.

Muriel Lester in India. (*Muriel Lester Collection of the Kingsley Halls' Heritage Committee*)

Ghandi arrives in the East End.

Hetty Bower meeting Ed Miliband. (*"Meeting Hetty Bower on International Women's Day (5509629274)" by Ed Miliband is licensed under CC BY 2.0.*)

Ellen Jones. (*Share UK photo by Elizabeth Dalziel*)

Anny Brackx. (*Share UK illustration by Laura Greenan*)

GLF London, 1972.

Jane (centre), Lynn and Rhi at London Pride 2014, staffing the LGSM stall.

Welsh miners march with LGSM at Pride. (*David Jones*)

Bangladeshi children in the East End.

Julie Begum (centre) and Women Unite Against Racism. (*Nurjahan Julie Begum*)

Sonali Bhattacharyya. (*Photo by Helen Murray*)

Claremont Road. (*Sheila Freeman*)

Reclaim the Streets, 1994. (*Ziggy Melamed*)

Faiza Shaheen.
(*Andy Sewell*)

Chapter 7

Hetty Rise Up!

Like many of today's London suburbs, early Hackney was a rural community with scattered hamlets, market gardens and rolling pastures where cattle grazed. The river Lea ran lazily through it, surrounded by open marsh land.

The first disruption came in 1707, when a mill opened at Lea Bridge. Harnessing the power of nature, water was used to bore holes in tree trunks to make water pipes, and grind corn. By the nineteenth century, the west bank of the river became lined with timber yards, providing wood for the burgeoning furniture industry. Grand houses were built for bankers and merchants seeking a rural retreat close to the city.

The arrival of the railways in the second half of the nineteenth century, brought the second disruption. Hackney's population grew rapidly, boosted, in part, by Jewish migrants fleeing the Russian pogroms. Those who'd found some prosperity move out of Whitechapel and into Dalston and Canonbury[1]; South Hackney received overspill from Bethnal Green and Stepney; while those with a bit more money move to Stamford Hill and Stoke Newington. By 1895, Hackney synagogue was serving a community 'thickly populated by the better class of Jewish working man.'[2]

Gabriel Rimel came into this community at the turn of the twentieth century. Unlike other Hackney Jews, Gabriel didn't escaped persecution in the Russian Empire. He was born in Austria, where Jews enjoyed relative prosperity and equality. His background may have set him apart, for although he originally settled in Whitechapel, he wasn't sucked into the grind of the sweat shops. Instead, he set up his own business as a food provisions merchant. In 1894, he married Manie (later known as Milly), also from Austria. Their first two children were born in Whitechapel, but by 1900 they'd moved to Colveston Crescent in Hackney, where their third child was born. According to Charles Booth's poverty maps, Colveston Crescent was a middle-class area 'harbouring many Jews' in houses of three-and-a-half stories, with small front gardens on wide, clean streets.[3]

Business was obviously good for Gabriel, as by 1911 they'd taken on a Russian migrant servant called Hannah. Her help must have come as a relief to Milly, who went on to have 10 children. That included Esther, known as Hetty, who was born in 1905.

While Gabriel was a radical Liberal, he was also an Orthodox Jew who didn't believe that women should be in politics. That didn't stop Hetty's older sister, Sisy, who snuck out the house to attend suffragette meetings. Her father's attitude didn't dissuade Hetty's curiosity either. She'd stay up waiting for Sisy to come home. Hearing the front door open, Hetty would check their father wasn't in sight, and tiptoe through the dark hallways to see her. 'Tell me everything,' she'd whisper.

Sisy recalled the rousing speeches by Sylvia Pankhurst, who explained how her father had started the campaign for votes for women. Not just the rich women either, but all women. Sylvia was carrying on the fight and urged the new recruits to throw themselves into the cause. She told them they'd have to be prepared to face anything, and that meant sometimes being in danger.[4] It was an ethos that would drive Hetty throughout her life.

Despite the Rimel's comfortable home and economic good fortune, Britain was becoming increasingly hostile for Jews. The year Hetty was born, the government passed the Aliens Act, which restricted the number of Jews who could settle in the country. It also made plain to those already here, they weren't wanted. A disturbing new campaign emerged through an organisation called the British Brothers' League. It described itself as 'anti alien', but there was little doubt who their main target was.[5] It enjoyed support from a number of MPs, and local media, galvanising poorer communities into angry marches around the East End. The response of many Jews was to keep their heads down and try to assimilate.

When war broke out, Hetty joined the patriotism, standing on the streets waving the men off to the frontlines. She saw those same men return with arms and legs missing, or totally blind. In an interview with the Stop the War Coalition, aged 108 years old, she could still remember the moment where it all changed for her:

> I was nine years old when World War 1 started, the so-called war to end all wars. In 1914 we were being subjected to lies and ferocious propaganda. Telling the British people lying horror stories, they injected fear. During war the real horror strikes you, and it leaves a scar that a child cannot forget. Men's legs and arms were blown off and I can recall, at age nine, asking … why? Nobody could give me a satisfactory answer. I remember the build up – The Lord Kitchener poster with his large index finger pointing – 'Britain Wants You, join the country's army. God Save The King!' But who saves the people? What do you mean your King needs you? For what? To die!

Yet within of the horrors of war a new loved emerged. Hetty remembers how music got her through the bombardments:

> We were told to get to the bottom of our houses […] Mother would call up from the bottom of the stairs – bring your pillows with you! We would bring our pillows down and sit at our enormous mahogany table. On top of that table my eldest sister's husband would bring an enormous HMV horn, on which we played records. That was the first time I heard Mozart and a Beethoven symphony; they were beautiful. It was the beginning of my love of music. It blocked out the sound of the war.[6]

By 15, the war had ended and Hetty had left school. She worked as an assistant to her father, alongside her older brother Israel and sister Annie. Yet she was also digging deeper into politics. In 1922, she went to the Queens Hall in Langham Place, which at the time was London's principal concert venue. From the cramped, stuffy hall she heard the election results announced live, as the first Labour MPs entered parliament.

The following year, age 17, Hetty joined the Labour Party herself. This positioned her as 'Jewish Labour and Jewish youth', a term used disparagingly by the older, wealthier Jewish community. These young radicals were typified as second generation migrants, who were largely divorced from the synagogue and uninterested in Jewish affairs. While the Jewish establishment thought it acceptable to assimilate into middle and upper class society, mixing with the poorer end of the population was highly undesirable.[7] This didn't stop Hetty.

One day, the Labour Party gave her a batch of leaflets with names of people who'd applied to join. She was told to go and meet them, and give them a warm welcome. Among that list was a man called Reg Bower, who was collecting money for the locked-out miners. Hetty remembers: 'My first reaction when I saw him was: what a pity he isn't a Jew, because he was very pleasant-looking and you couldn't help but respond to that smile!'[8]

Reg was born in 1906, also in Dalston, but later moved to Bromley-by-Bow, where he lived with his mother, two sisters and step-father. He worked as a junior clerk at James and Co Chartered Accountants. Hetty wouldn't know it then, but they would spend the next 70 years campaigning together.

The General Strike

On 4th May 1926, Hetty got up with Sisy at 4am to make sandwiches and hot drinks for the strikers on the picket lines. They thought they were being quiet, when the kitchen door burst open. Their mother glared at them: 'What do you think you are doing at this time in the morning?' she demanded.

The girls exchanged nervous looks. 'But Mummy! We have to feed the strikers.'

Their mother scowled. 'Of course they need to be fed, but you're absolutely not going out alone at this time in the morning.' At which point their younger brother was woken and made to escort his two sisters to the picket line.[9]

Hetty was stirred into action by the plight of the miners, whose strike was at the centre of the dispute. At the Friday night Hackney Labour Party meeting, a speaker from the Rhonda Valley described the hardship the miners were suffering. The speaker broke down in tears as he explained the conditions of starving families. Hetty was incredibly moved. She'd never seen a grown man cry before.

As in Bow, workers in Hackney came out in solidarity with the miners. The usual bustling Kingsland Road was virtually empty, with not a bus or tram in sight. There was such hope – they were going to save the miners – yet ten days later that hope turned to despair.

The general strike is often depicted as a failure, and a humiliation for the TUC, but Hetty saw things differently. 'I never thought it was a waste of time,' she said, remembering the strike over 80 years later. 'It made a lot of people aware of what the miners did.'[10]

The rise Mosely and the Blackshirts

Hetty got over her disappointment of Reg not being a Jew, and in 1932 they married. But beyond their personal happiness, the world grew darker. Throughout the 30s, Jews in Britain experienced a wide range of antisemitic incidents, including physical attacks on people and property. Smashing windows of Jewish owned and Jewish frequented shops was common, as well as antisemitic slogans gratified on pavements and walls. Job adverts in shop windows and newspapers often specified that they would not hire Jews, and insurance companies considered them 'bad risks' and 'untrustworthy'.[11] Finding housing could be an issue, with Jews excluded from certain flats. In Walthamstow, East London, a property company denied Jews access to a block of flats, on the ground that its gentile tenants disliked having Jewish neighbours. Those looking for a seaside break were often met with signs at resorts specifying 'no dogs, no Jews.'[12]

Out of this atmosphere emerged the British Union of Fascists (BUF), whose membership peaked in 1934 at 40,000 members. Its leader, Sir Oswald Mosely, was born into an aristocratic family, and educated at Winchester Public School and Sandhurst. In 1918, he moved into politics, winning a seat for the Conservatives in Harrow. During his time in parliament, he'd flit through both the Conservatives and the Labour

Party, before starting the unimaginatively titled, New Party. Modelled on Benito Mussolini's fascist movement in Italy, in October 1932 it transformed into the BUF.

High unemployment, and a government that lacked confidence in dealing with the crisis, boosted the BUF. In the early 30s, unemployment figures reached three million, with a third of the population out of work in several major industrial areas. People looked for someone to blame, and Mosely had the answer.

Building on working class discontent, Mosley focused his activities in areas surrounding Jewish communities, including in Manchester, Leeds and East London. He organised public meetings, mass rallies, demonstrations and distributed leaflets and pamphlets. The rallies became notorious for Mosely's bodyguards, known as the Blackshirts after Musollini's paramilitary wing. They brutally put down any opposition. The BUF also enjoyed support from Viscount Rothermere of The Daily Mail, who on 15th January 1934, declared on its front page: "Hurrah for the Blackshirts".

Despite the dangerous rise in antisemitism, many Jewish community leaders continued to see it as something that happened in other European countries. They believed British society would set firm boundaries to stop it escalating. That included the Board of Deputies, the official voice of Jews in Britain. Then, as now, the Board of Deputies only represented a certain section of the community. They were completely disconnected from Jewish Labour, Jewish youth, Jewish trade unions and secular Jews. As the threat from the BUF grew, this wider Jewish community urged the Board of Deputies to act. Yet the Jewish Chronicle, which was closely aligned with the official leadership, continued to tell its readers to act with constraint.[13]

The BUF's activities escalated. In March 1936, Herbert Morrison, MP for Hackney South, gave a speech in the House of Commons during a debate on anti semitism. He said:

There is a case of a man living in Stoke Newington who was attacked by a gang of Blackshirts in December while walking along Hackney

Downs at 11.45pm, and a friend was so badly knocked about that he was obliged to receive hospital treatment for two weeks. These people are spreading the slogans, 'Kill the Jews' and 'Dirty Jews', and so on in the neighbourhood, and are actually affixing to various places… a gummed slip with 'Jew' on it, and other slips with the Hitler trademark, the Swastika, in the middle and the words 'Perish Judah'. That is obviously action which is stimulating a breach of security of His Majesty's subjects […] it is obvious that action of that kind is calculated to […] inflame racial hatred in a district where clearly, it is particularly undesirable that that should be done […] we simply cannot tolerate a situation in which these people are taking the law into their own hands and making the Jews feel, when they go on to the King's highway, that they are not safe from molestation.[14]

On 26th September 1936, the BUF announced its plans to celebrate the organisation's fourth anniversary, with a parade of four marching columns. The march was designed to go through the heart of London's East End, in a deliberate provocation of the 60,000 strong Jewish population.

With agitation growing, a new grassroots organisation formed called the Jewish People's Council Against Fascism and Antisemitism (JPC). They launched a petition calling on the secretary of state to ban the BUF march, collecting over 100,000 signatures. On 1st October, a deputation of five East End mayors met with Home Office officials, to express their fears if the march proceeded. The Home Office refused to intervene, but agreed to despatch 7000 police officers to maintain order.

Three days before the proposed march, the ILP toured with a van and loud speakers through the streets of the East End. They called on people to come in their thousands to block all entry points. The appeal was reported on the front page of The Evening Standard, London's daily newspaper, and at a large indoor anti-fascist rally in Hackney. The following day, a 4000 strong anti-fascist march went from Tower Hill to the East End. They handed out leaflets, calling on people to oppose 'fascist hooligans in East London.'[15]

Meanwhile, the Jewish Chronicle urged Jews to keep away, warning that any involvement in public disorders would be aiding antisemitism. The Board of Deputies appealed for restraint through the synagogues. Some of the liberal press, including the Daily Herald, also told people to stay at home. All this advice was ignored.[16]

The Battle of Cable Street

By 1.30pm on Sunday 4th October, in a show of mass solidarity, around 10,000 Jews, Communists, and Irish dockers gathered in the East End. Using packing cases, fish boxes from nearby Billingsgate Market, timber, corrugated iron and even an overturned lorry, they blocked all the main streets around Aldgate.

Over at Tower Hill, Mosely and his Blackshirts lined up, waiting for the police to clear a path. They cut a menacing figure in their new military uniform of black shirt with silver buttons, riding breeches with big buckles, and a peaked cap with the fascist lightning bolt symbol. London felt on the verge of civil war.

Back in Aldgate, chaos erupted. Police blew whistles and swung truncheons, cracking heads open as they pushed through the crowds of anti-fascist protestors. Hundreds lay bruised and bleeding, as ambulances screamed through the streets. Van loads of police reinforcements roared in, as dockers with pick axes pulled up paving slabs to secure the barricades. Men and young people climbed onto of roof tops, yelling anti-fascists slogans. On the ground a young man, with blood running down his face, held his fist aloft and shouted: 'Down with Mosely; down with the murderers'[17] People screamed and some threw lighted fireworks, as police charged their horses into the crowds. Labour activist, Beattie Orwell, saw protestors throwing marbles under their hooves, and they reared and twisted, throwing off their riders. She recalled: 'People were shouting, "they shall not pass". There were people from everywhere, dockers, communists, everybody was there. And the police, you couldn't move across the road because there were so many.'[18]

Joyce Goodman was only 12 years old in 1936. Growing up on Brady Street in Whitechapel, she'd seen the highly charged rent strikes, often led by local wives and mothers. She'd also been thrown out of her local Jewish youth club for selling Challenge, an anti-fascist newspaper by the Young Communist League. She remembers the horror of that day: 'We never saw a fascist. We were fighting the police. They were just hitting everyone. There were women going down under the horses' hooves. Absolute terror.'[19]

Beattie and Joyce were far from the only woman there. Hetty Bower was back in London after travelling around Europe with Reg. They'd attended the International Workers' Olympiad, an alternative to the Olympic Games, organised by socialist sports groups. Now the fight was on her doorstep. There's no account of her experiences on Cable Street that day, other than stating she wasn't on the frontline, but 'second to frontline'.[20] It's possible she was underplaying her part, as other witness accounts confirm that women were in the thick of it, playing a significant role.

Charlie Goodman, a young Jewish tailor and communist, witnessed incredible acts of bravery by women. Unable to get through the main streets, the Police Commissioner turned his attention to Cable Street, an extremely narrow road populated by mainly Jewish families in overcrowded housing. Charlie remembers: 'The women in the tenement buildings picked up everything they could lay their hands on and threw them at the police … the police ran into the sheds and the women came down from the tenements and bashed the doors in and the police came out with their hands up.'[21]

The importance of women on the frontlines of Cable Street was echoed by local communist activist, Phil Piratin: 'It was along Cable Street that from the roofs and the upper floors, people, ordinary housewives, and elderly women too, were throwing down milk bottles and other weapons and all kinds of refuse that they didn't any longer want in the house onto the police.'[22]

Women were among the 79 anti-fascists arrested that day, many of whom faced terrible brutality by the police. One woman was dragged into the station by a huge officer. He ripped off her blouse and held up his truncheon, as if to strike her. She looked him directly in the eye and said 'I am not scared of you.' The room went quiet, he called her a 'Jewish bitch' and threw her in a cell.[23]

Around 3pm, Fenner Brockway, secretary of the ILP and former MP for Leyton, called the Home Secretary, Sir John Simon. He wasn't available so Fenner left a message saying that 'if they did not stop or at least divert the procession, theirs would be the responsibility'.[24] By late afternoon there was still no response from the Home Office, so the police commissioner took matters into his own hands. He told Mosely to turn back. Mosely was furious, but had to comply. He'd long told his members to follow law and order. They didn't go quietly however, yelling 'Jewboy Simon's got the wind-up' and spitting at and taunting anyone of Jewish appearance.[25]

When the news came that the fascists had turned back, Beattie Orwell said a huge cheer went up. The anti-fascists marched up to Victoria Park, singing and shouting, 'they shall not pass'. They gathered for a huge rally to celebrated their incredible victory.[26]

The aftermath

Following the so-called Battle of Cable Street, questions were asked as to how such horror could occur. The Daily Mirror questioned the Home secretary why the march wasn't banned. They gave no clear reason, but denied fearing restrictions on freedom of speech. Two days later, MPs called for a ban on political uniforms. Within three weeks a Public Order Bill was prepared. It came into force in January 1937. It banned political uniforms, gave extended powers to the police to restrict processions, and increased the maximum penalty for insulting, threatening or abusive behaviours.[27]

The Act was broadly welcomed by the public, and the Board of Deputies. The Daily Mirror ran a statement from Mosely, saying 'The British Government has openly surrendered to the Red Terror.'[28] Meanwhile, those on the left complained that the government appeared to blame both sides. This is reminiscent of Donald Trump in 2017, following violence in Charlottesville where an anti-racist protestor was killed.

Towards the end of the 1930s, growing hostility towards Nazi Germany saw BUF membership decline. The Government finally banned the party in May 1940, following the outbreak of WW2, and growing suspicions that remaining supporters might form a pro-Nazi fifth column.

World War Two

On 3rd September 1939, Hetty's father told her: 'Oh, they've declared war! Now the lies will begin.'[29] Hetty still felt there was no logic in military conflict; no good reason for humans killing each other.

While Hackney was not in the epicentre, it still received a significant amount of bomb damage. Unlike its neighbouring boroughs, there were no tube stations to shelter in. It was not uncommon to go to bed one night, and wake up the next morning to find your neighbour's house, with all the inhabitants, gone.[30]

Despite the chaos around her, Hetty remained a committed internationalist, focusing particularly on Czechoslovakia. During the 1930s, Prague had a flourishing Jewish community. When Hitler came to power in Germany, many more arrived as refugees. In 1939, Germany invaded, and between 1941–1945, over 46,000 Jews were deported from the city to a ghetto in Theresiendstadt[31]. From here, they were transported to Auschwitz for extermination. Back in East Finchley, Hetty volunteered at a refugee hostel for 'trade unionists, socialists, communists, Jews, and anyone else they could get out of Czechoslovakia.'[32] She made such an impact, she ended up running the whole operation.

On 6th August, the first atomic bomb dropped on the Japanese city of Hiroshima. Three days later, a second dropped on Nagasaki. Hundreds of thousands lost their lives. The atomic age had begun.

CND and the nuclear threat

In the 1950s, Europe was gripped in fear of nuclear conflict. In a mass public meeting in February 1958, the Campaign for Nuclear Disarmament

(CND) launched. It attracted people from all walks of society, from scientists all too well aware of the dangers posed; to religious leaders. The Quakers were supportive, as were Labour Party members and trade unionists. Having survived two world wars already, Hetty Bower was one of the first to join its campaign for multilateral disarmament.

The following Easter weekend, CND organised a mass march. It went from the Atomic Weapons Research Establishment in Aldermaston in Berkshire, to London, a distance of 52 miles, taking the nuclear disarmament message to the heart of government. Thousands participated, and it became an annual event. At its peak in the 1960s, the march attracted 40,000 people, and 100,000 attended the final rally in Trafalgar Square. Jo Richardson was an organiser on three of the marches, and later a Labour MP. She explained: 'Everyone was there to show their opposition to the bomb: organisers, caterers, drivers and, above all, marchers. That's why there really were no cross words and no problems that couldn't eventually be solved, in that marvellous spirit of comradeship which is my abiding memory of the Easter Marches.'[33]

Hetty was there on the first march, and 50 years later was still marching. Her only complaint was that people didn't walk fast enough. 'Why shouldn't I march,' the centenarian said. 'I've got good legs!'[34]

The Iraq War

On 11th September 2001, Al-Qaeda carried out four coordinated terror attacks against the United States. Governments worldwide denounced the strikes, including in the middle east. Prime Minister, Tony Blair, flew to Washington to affirm British solidarity with the US. NATO declared that attacks on the US were an attack on all NATO nations. The US government announced a 'war on terror', with the aim of bringing Al-Qaeda to justice.

In the immediate aftermath of 9/11, the US government rejected the idea of attacking Iraq. By early 2002, President Bush insisted the invasion was necessary, due to Saddam Hussein violating the United Nations (UN) resolution on weapons of mass destruction. He argued there were links between Hussein and Al-Qaida. This, he maintained, meant Iraq posed a significant and imminent threat to the US.

The proposed war was deeply controversial, especially as evidence of these weapons of mass destruction seemed vague. Over a two year period, 1,625 UN and US inspectors searched 1,700 sites, at a cost of $1bn. They reported that Saddam Hussein destroyed his last weapons of mass destruction more than a decade before. Although Hussein told his interrogators he had ambitions to restart a chemical and nuclear programme once sanctions were lifted, there were no concrete plans. No paperwork was found and none of Hussein's closest aides knew about it. Hussein said his desire to re-arm was driven primarily by a fear of Iran and its nuclear capabilities. The inspectors described Hussein as a 'dwindling threat'. A separate leaked CIA report found no link between Baghdad and Al-Qaida.[35] Despite this, in 2003 troops were sent in to disarm Iraq of its weapons, and remove Hussein and his Baath Party from government.

Nearly two-thirds of Americans thought that the Iraqi government had something to do with the 9/11 attacks.[36] Globally there was more hesitation. In a poll of 41 countries, around half were not in favour of military action against Iraq under any circumstances. This feeling was particularly strong in Spain (74%) and France (60%).[37]

Around the world, anti-war protestors organised. They called for a global day of action on 15th February 2003. In the UK, this was coordinated by the Stop The War Coalition. They'd formed two weeks after the 9/11 attacks, when President Bush announced his war on terror. They were dedicated to opposing British involvement in conflicts in the middle east, and the establishment's 'disastrous addiction to war and its squandering of public resources on militarism.'[38]. Amongst its sponsors were Labour MPs, Tony Benn, George Galloway and Jeremy Corbyn, as well as author and journalist, Tariq Ali, playwright, Harold Pinter, and leading trade unionists.

As the event approached, it became clear it was going to be bigger than anyone anticipated. Thousands booked coaches to London from all parts of the country. Due to its size, two separate starting points were organised: Thames Embankment for Londoners and those travelling from the south; and Gower Street for those travelling from the midlands and North. The two marches merged at Piccadilly Circus, and proceeded to a rally at Hyde Park. Media coverage leading up to the event painted a picture of a nation rising up. Many citizens getting on buses were attending their first protest, such was the level of outrage. A number of those were young people finding a political identity; others were older, and didn't see themselves as activists. And then there was Hetty Bower, now nearly 100 years old, who'd been marching all her life.

On that grey, extremely cold day in February, she marched alongside her two daughters – Margie and Celia – and an estimated million others.[39] Despite the number of historic events she'd been part of, this was by far the largest. In an ICM poll for The Guardian, 6% of people claimed that someone from their household went on the march or had intended to. Parts of central London became gridlocked with protestors. Despite the grim weather, people remained cheerful, with chanting, singing and dancing to music blaring from loud speakers (something Hetty was less keen on).

Yet even with these huge numbers, war wasn't averted. On 19th March 2003, the United Kingdom began its military operations in Iraq. Journalist and activist, Ellie Mae O'Hagan claimed that the protest 'did absolutely nothing', while Tariq Ali said that despite the huge show of public anger it 'left no lasting legacy'.[40] However Seumas Milne, journalist and political aide under Jeremy's Corbyn's Labour Party, said: 'If people imagine one demonstration is going to change everything of course that's wrong, but demos, protests, social organisation, trade union organisation, political organisation – all these things are part of the process by which things are going to shift.'[41]

Although only a small sample, oral history interviews conducted as part of the Women Activists of East London project[42], support Milne's point. While the 2003 Iraq war march didn't achieve its main objective, it acted as a trigger point for many who were there. During those interviews it was cited several times as a first taste of activism, especially amongst millennial women. They'd continue to mobilise in other actions, including the 2010 student protests and 2018 women's march.

The Iraq war was a turning point for Hetty Bower too. Despite being a Labour Party member for over 80 years, she resigned her membership. In an interview with the Stop The War Coalition she didn't mince her words: 'Tony Blair is a Catholic. How can he believe in God when he killed so many people? He's a liar and he sold propaganda.'

Nobody knows better than Hetty Bower that it will always take more than one protest to change anything. In the 10 years following 2003 protest, she marched nearly 30 times to oppose war, nuclear weapons, and against Israel's oppression of the Palestinians. In 2008, age 102 years old she was still fighting for peace, speaking at the Hiroshima Commemoration Day in Tavistock Square. At 106, she walked three miles in St Albans, Hertfordshire to raise money for Palestinian children in Oxfam's Annual Herts Hike.

Hetty was an impressive orator, speaking clearly, although slightly too loudly due to some hearing loss. She sometimes gave the impression of sternness, but she also loved to laugh. Speaking invites rolled in from universities and political rallies. She felt a particular passion for educating the next generation, visiting a number of local schools. She explained:

In my room I have a wonderful new year's card from the children at Highgate Primary School. I was asked to come and talk to the children about what school was like when I was a child. There were two small 8-year-old boys that kept persistently asking me questions about the First World War. They asked which one was worse, World War One or World War Two? So I responded by asking, why this fascination with war and with killing each other? What made it so interesting? So, I thought I would turn it around and ask them: why do adults kill each other? They were confused, they didn't know how to deal with me.

That new year I received a wonderful card for peace that the children all signed. I take their card to every commemoration. When I go and commemorate Hiroshima and Nagasaki; these are things that should never, ever have happened. Lest we forget, lest we forget – I will not forget Hiroshima, the start of nuclear war.[43]

Hetty didn't limit herself to the peace campaign. In 2010, she marched against the closure of her local Whittingham Hospital, where her daughter Margie was born, and she received a hip replaced by its surgeons. She could remember it from the pre-NHS days, as a workhouse infirmary. These were established in the nineteenth century to provide free medical care to workhouse residents. Originally nursing was done by other inmates, many of whom could not read. By Hetty's day there were paid nurses, but only one nurse to around 20 patients. Having seen Britain before and after the welfare state, she was an outspoken critic of government austerity. She joined the Real Britain campaign, alongside poverty campaigner, Jack Munroe, and Unite general secretary, Len McCluskey.

In 2013, she spoke at the Labour Party conference, stealing the show. Leaving barely a dry eye in the house she spoke about the days before the NHS with painful clarity. 'Families were forced to choose between buying medicine for their children, or a loaf of bread,' she remembered. 'We must never ever go back to those days." She told the conference delegates that whatever time she had left on this planet she would dedicated to the fight, urging them to do the same. 'We may not win,' she said 'But if we do not protest we will lose.'[44] Her speech received a standing ovation.

At the conference, Jack Munroe was thrilled to meet her lifelong hero. She told Hetty she wanted to be her when she grew up, which made Hetty roar with laughter. In her blog, Jack said: 'You told me to keep fighting for what I believe in. And I will. I may not make it to 108, but I will protest until I die.'[45]

A few months after the Labour Party conference, Hetty had a stroke as she was about to leave home to speak at a primary school. As she lay in hospital with her family around her, she sung the old CND standard, The H-Bomb's Thunder. Wagging her finger, she said: 'Ban the bomb, forever more.' At 108 years old, they were her final words.

Hetty's legacy

In an obituary by The Mirror, the journalist writes that Hetty would've probably disapproved of the article, as she didn't like reading about herself.

The same article describes her as shy. Yet other articles describe her as stern and outspoken. So maybe this perceived shyness was something else?

Hetty was a committed socialist. She believed in the power of collective action, not individual heroics. It was within these movements that she found victory. In solidarity with the dockers and communists, she pushed back the fascists on the streets of Aldgate; with comrades in North London she saved the lives of Jews and others in Czechoslovakia; and marching through London with a million others, she inspired a new generation of young people. Maybe this is why she didn't want the focus on her.

Hetty also believed in the power of intergenerational action. Shortly before her death, she gave a talk at an East End secondary school. The mainly Muslim pupils were staging a musical about the Battle of Cable Street. She told them: 'Now it's up to your generation to stand against fascism and racism.'[46]

While world peace was not achieved within Hetty's lifetime, she probably always knew that. Like many women, she fought for her children and grandchildren, and the world she would leave behind.

Sadly, life for her daughter Margie would be a short one. Five years after Hetty died, Margie was killed in a cycling accident. A week before she'd been with a friend to the Women's March in London. They'd ended their day at the Millicent Fawcett statue in Parliament Square, commemorating the suffragist movement many generations earlier. Margie brought her mother along with her – in the form of her face on a t-shirt.[47] The three generations at Parliament Square that day shows it's not always about the winning, but the resistance; and how we pass the fight on to the next generation. As Tony Benn once said: 'There is no final victory, and there is no final defeat. There is just the same battle to be fought over and over. So toughen up. Bloody toughen up.'

Part III

1970–1990

Chapter 8

Ellen Rise Up!

Ellen rolled over in her sleeping bag, shivering. She reached down for her hot water bottle – it was a solid lump of ice. Wrapping a blanket around herself, she opened the door of the bender tent, and it creaked as the snow fell off. Outside, everything looked like it was covered in a white bed sheet.

A few other people were up, and huddled around the fire pit, white wisps of smoke dancing through the air. The kettle rattled, as water inside bubbled. Ellen grabbed a vaguely clean cup and held it out as one of her fellow sisters filled it up, steam rising into her face. She muttered a thank you, and held the hot tin to her lips. God, it was cold!

Ellen knew the only way to get through days like these was to keep active. So she popped her bolt cutters in her pocket, and began the nine mile walk around the perimeter fence. Up ahead she could see a solider, gun gripped in his hand. It was probably the same one she saw there most mornings. As she walked by, she let out a cheery 'good morning'. She didn't expect him to reply; he never did. Except for that one time, but she thought that might have been a mistake. She'd caught him off guard and he'd momentarily forgotten she was the enemy. She'd tried striking up a conversation.

'Why are you here? she'd asked.

'Excuse me, Ma'am?'

'Why did you join the army? To see the world? And you ended up in Newbury, huh?'

He hadn't replied.

Today it was too cold to stop, so she kept walking.

'Ma'am?'

Ellen turned and saw the solider holding something out to her.

'Would you like a cup of tea?' he asked.

'Yes, sure,' she replied, walking back.

He poured the hot liquid from his thermos into the little plastic cup. He went to passed it to her, forgetting there was a wire fence between them. The cup smashed against it, tea sloshing over the sides.

'Oh let me,' Ellen said, taking the bolt cutters from her pocket. She snipped at the chains in the fence, and peeled back the wire flap.

The solider passed the cup through.

Ellen gulped it down, and gave it back to him. He took it without a word, and walked away.

It would be nice to say this was the start of a new relationship, but it wasn't. They never spoke again. But at least he now knew she was a human being, so maybe when the trouble started … because there was bound to be more trouble. There always was on the Greenham Common Women's Peace Camp.[1]

Camp beginnings

In September 1981, a group of 36 women, and a few male supporters, marched 120 miles from Cardiff, to the RAF Greenham Common air base near Newbury in Berkshire. Calling themselves, Women for Life on Earth, they marked their arrival with brightly coloured scarves, flowers, ribbons, and one woman doing somersaults. They delivered a letter to the Base Commander requesting a meeting to discuss the expected arrival of US nuclear missiles. The airbase was on common land, loaned to the Americans by the British Government during WW2, but never returned to the people of Newbury. Each of the nuclear missiles they planned to stored there was four times the power of the bomb that destroyed Hiroshima. There were hundreds expected to arrive. One MP said: 'There will be enough cruise nuclear missiles to destroy the world.'[2]

When the Commander refused to meet, the group remained at the base and set up a peace camp. The Commander said they could stay for as long as they wanted, for all he cared. So they stayed 19 years.

Peace camps weren't new. There's evidence of Quaker peace camps in southern England as early as the 1930s. Hetty Bower stayed on a socialist camp when she and Reg visited the International Workers Olympiad in 1936. In 1958, CND's Direct Action Committee set up a temporary camp following the first Aldermaston march. It remained outside the Atomic Weapons Research Establishment that whole summer.[3] But Women for Life on Earth took the peace camp to a whole new level, making it a campaigning tactic within itself.

In February 1982, the camp became women only. The activists foregrounded their identity as mothers, and their goal of creating a safer world for their children. They attached pictures of their kids to the airbase fence, wearing black and lighting candles to mourn their children's futures.

Nicky Skinner was inspired to join the peace camp because of her children. She said: 'My motivation was my overriding safety and unease about the safety for my children. Greenham Common is within 100 miles of us, if anything were fired at Greenham, where the missiles were stored, then it wouldn't just be Greenham that got hit. It would spread out to Portsmouth.'[4]

Another reason the camp became women only was because some felt the men were not doing enough work. They also feared that during demonstrations the men were more likely to become aggressive. The women wanted all actions to be non-violent. Eventually they told the men to leave. It didn't go down well. Some stormed off the site. But while the women succeeded in making the protest their own, another patriarchal attack was coming.[5]

The public response

Media coverage in the beginning was disappointing. Then four women chained themselves to the fence. They were first in what would become a regular rota. Once the media latched on to what was happening, the coverage increased but it wasn't always positive. They largely ignored the existential threat the women were fighting against, focusing instead on their behaviour. They asked why they weren't at home looking after their children, and described the camp as a witches coven.[6]

Locally, the women faced hostility too. Pubs refused to serve them, some vigilante groups physically attacked them, and there were rape and death threats. There was also police brutality and harassment. Ellen was on the camp for around two years. During that time she was spat at when getting food supplies; thrown in a ditch by military police; picked up and accidentally dropped on her head, knocking her unconscious; and lay in the middle of the road singing protest songs, hoping the police horses wouldn't step on her.

Life before the camp

Ellen was born in Aberystwyth, on the west coast of Wales. It was a quiet life – too quiet for Ellen. She was a child of the 60s. She went to art college and had a long-haired boyfriend her parents disapproved of. She was eager for more excitement in her life. As a teenager, she watched the Vietnam War protests on TV, and saw Nelson Mandela fighting apartheid. When her friends at school joined CND, she signed up with them.

While at art college, she met her husband. They moved to Swansea, and joined the local CND group. The Swansea group was very active, as its members felt they had to fight to protect such a beautiful part of the world. They held meetings, put up posters and invited speakers. When they heard about the nuclear missiles coming to RAF Greenham Common, things heated up.

In March 1982, a vigil was organised on the Greenham Common peace camp. Ellen remembers: 'I'd heard so much about [the peace camp], but I just felt like reading about it in the newspaper wasn't enough anymore. I had to go there and find out for myself what was going on.'

So a group of the Swansea women got a van and headed to the Berkshire military base. 'It was amazing,' Ellen said. 'I thought there would be around 50 or so women, but thousands turned up. I had this really strong feeling that this was where I was supposed to be.'

Ellen returned a few months later, along with 30,000 other women. Their aim was to create a human chain around the base, in what became known as Embrace the Base. Supporters came from all over Britain, and America, Africa, Asia and New Zealand. Among them were a number of high profile figures, including Yoko Ono, Sheila Hancock, Julie Christie, Glynnis and Neil Kinnock and Michael Foot.

Ellen remembers:

There was a nine mile perimeter fence. We were sent to different gates. Each gate was given a different colour of the rainbow. I remember mine was orange. More and more women kept coming, and then we were all told to link hands. The nine miles was surrounded and there was this amazing sound. Then we all put pictures, flowers, peace flags on to the fence. It was an amazing feeling.

When Ellen returned from the camp this time, something felt different. She didn't know what she was doing back home when a nuclear attack could end the world at any time. She had to get back to Greenham. So in 1983, she headed in for a third visit. This time she stayed for two years.

Life on the camp

Daily life on the camp was tough. There were no proper toilets or washing facilities, and no permanent shelters. They slept in sleeping bags in tents made from tree branches and plastic. Although you never got much sleep because of the constant noise and light around the base. There was also the need to keep the camp functioning, with things like regular water and food supplies. Somebody would take charge of cooking, and everyone else did the washing up.

When winter came so did the gales and mud. It looked like the Somme. Many women went back to their families, but others, like Ellen, stayed, taking on the constant fight against the cold. She recalled:

I did an interview from Greenham in the snow for Welsh television, for S4C, for the news. I didn't think any more of it. Next time I went home, this neighbour said, "Oh, I saw you on television and it was all amazing." I didn't know they'd recognise me with my layers and layers of clothes, but obviously they did. My mother was horrified.

She was just so embarrassed. But then she bought me a whole bunch of thermal vests to take back with me. I've still got one of them. I can't bear to throw it away.

This daily grind was punctuated with the high intensity of direct actions. One of the most famous was in October 1983, when they took down four miles of the fence. Ellen and a group of women went to Wales to buy some extra-large bolt cutters. They had some money for a deposit, and were warned they would lose it if they weren't returned. Ellen remembers:

We went back to Greenham, and there was this mass surrounding of the fence. At a particular moment, everybody just cut, and sections of the fence collapsed. We all got arrested at that point – when I say all, I can't remember how many, but an awful lot of women got arrested. Of course, they took our bolt cutters.

A month or so later, I went back to the shop in Wales, and I said to the guy: "Really sorry, but I haven't got your bolt cutters." And he was like, "Oh, blah, blah, blah, your deposit, you're going to lose your deposit". He said, "What happened to the bolt cutters?" I said, "Oh, we were at Greenham…" And he stopped, and said, "Was it that thing that was in the newspaper?" And I said, "Well, yes possibly." He said, "Where a load of women …" He said, "Oh, never mind the deposit, love." And that was that, got away with it.

In August 1982, women got on to the base itself, occupying a sentry box. This led to arrest, court and sentencing. They didn't stop there. The following year, 44 women used ladders to climb on to the base. They were also arrested and sent to court. The judge refused bail, and the women went to Holloway prison, where the suffragettes, Poplar women councillors, and Muriel Lester had been before them. Rather than singing The Red Flag, the Greenham activists had their own anthem, You Can't Kill the Spirit.

You can't kill the Spirit
She is like a mountain
Old and strong
She goes on an on and on[7]

Sometimes the police didn't know what to do with the women. Ellen explains:

> There were times when you'd get arrested, and you'd get bundled into a van, and you'd end up in a police station. But they didn't know what to do with you because there was so many of us. I was once taken to Newbury Court, but there were hundreds of women; they couldn't deal with it. I don't even remember if I got fined. I don't think I did … I did end up with a criminal record. It said "urban terrorist" and in brackets "not IRA".

In November 1983, the missiles arrived. The women had failed to stop them, but they had triggered a national debate. And they weren't giving up. Three weeks after the arrival of the weapons, 50,000 women circled the airbase. In silence, they held up mirrors to allow the base to symbolically looked back on itself, and its actions. The day ended in more arrests as women pulled down large sections of the fence again.[8]

Following the arrival of the weapons, the police response intensified. The Conservative government was determined to get rid of the women. Secretary for Defence, Michael Heseltine, warned the women they could be shot if they trespassed on the base.

Yet the women continued to get inside. One group climbed into the control tower. Some looked through the nuclear and biological weapons manuals, and wrote peace messages in them. Others wrote on the walls. A solider discovered them. He pulled out his gun, but lost his nerve. Police arrested them, but later dropped all charges.[9]

That same year, CND organised tens of thousands of protestors in a human chain. Stretching 14 miles, it linked the Greenham peace camp with the Aldermaston nuclear research centre, where their annual peace walk departs from. They called the route, nuclear valley. CND claimed around 80,000 people took part, including the actress Julie Christie. After completing the peace chain, they held a rally at Aldermaston.[10]

Meanwhile, local actions emerged around the country, including in Hackney, East London. In February 1984, women supporters set up their own camp outside Hackney Town Hall. They put on an exhibition showing the horrors of nuclear destruction, and organised picnics, music and camp fires in the evening. The following year, the Dalston Lane Peace Mural was created. Led by Ray Walker and painted by Mike Jones and Anna Walker, it depicts a parade through a Hackney streetscape, containing anti-nuclear, CND, anti-war, green, feminist, anti-racist, and pro-tolerance images. This well-loved local landmark remains today as a powerful reminder of the peace movement in Hackney.

The Hackney camp generated a lot of support from the local community, and membership of the Hackney Greenham group increased rapidly. In September that year, several coaches took women from Hackney to Greenham Common.

Eviction

In 1982, Newbury Council made their first eviction attempt, but a new camp was set up within days. In April 1985, the Ministry of Defence invoked by-laws on trespass. There were court battles and arrests. Bulldozers arrived, and the women lay down in front of them and climbed into the cabs. Police and bailiffs turned up, and the women set fire to their tents in protest. Every time they clear the camp, the women returned by nightfall and re-established it. By 1987, parliament was told the camp was finally cleared, but women still returned every night and cut down parts of the fence. They also set up nine smaller camps at various gates around the base. This group of women, unaffiliated to any political organisation, was a major embarrassment, not only to the British and US, but to the whole of NATO.

In 1985, Mikhail Gorbachev came to power in the Soviet Union. He committed to cutting down the world's dependence on nuclear weapons.

International nuclear disarmament talks began with the US and UK, resulting in the Intermediate-Range Nuclear Forces Treaty. In 1989, the first of the cruise missiles were removed from Greenham Common.

While the women welcome the move, they remained sceptical. By this time, the camp was more than about peace – it symbolised the women's struggle. For many it was a shelter from their difficult home lives. But for Ellen, she'd had enough. 'I think you can only do so much of it. It was strange though …. I don't think my life's been the same since.'

After leaving Greenham, Ellen lived in a caravan in mid-west Wales, to readjust to life back in society. She then moved to East London, where she remains today. For a while she carried on the fight, taking a job at CND headquarters. Today she makes jewellery, inspired by her time in the peace movement.

Ellen retains powerful memories of her time on the peace camp:

> You couldn't match it ever. There were arguments, there were rows, there was, "Who's getting the water? Who's doing this?" And then there was this incredible camaraderie as well. If you were breaking down a fence or running in front of a truck or something, everybody would help everybody.

In 1991, the last of the cruise missiles were removed from RAF Greenham Common. The Americans announced they were no longer using it as an operational base. But questions remained around what to do with the land. For many years a struggle continued between the Ministry for Defence and the people of Newbury, who demanded return of the common land. In 1997, the government finally gave it back to the community.

Following a New Year's Eve party in December 1999, the last of the campers left the site. In 2000, the fences surrounding the base were removed, and a memorial created to honour the anti-nuclear movement. It consists of a garden with Welsh standing stones surrounding a sculpture of a campfire. It's engraved with the words: 'You can't kill the spirit.' It officially opened in October 2002.[11]

The Greenham legacy

The Greenham Common women's peace camp kept the debate going about nuclear missiles throughout the 80s, raising the issue in the consciousness of the media, government and general public. Although changing international relationships was one of the biggest factors in the bases' closure, Gorbachev referenced the importance of the Greenham women's protest.[12]

The Greenham peace camp continues to hold iconic status. When Ellen mentions she was there, it amazes younger generations, who treat her like a rock star. Not just the women, but men too.

Greenham gained national and international status in terms of its innovation and campaigning creativity. Peace camps continued around Britain well after it ended. As the nuclear threat diminished, and environmental concerns grew, organisations like Climate Camp employed similar tactics. The Occupy movement also borrowed from it following the 2008 financial crisis.

In 2023, Palestine solidarity activists established a peace camp in Hackney, calling for a ceasefire in Gaza and an end to the illegal occupation. It stood outside the town hall, in the same place as the Hackney Greenham Common camp over 40 years earlier.

Chapter 9

Anny Rise Up!

'I have come to recognise that I belong to some incurable breed, and that life is a black hole with no future.'[1]

Anny closed her diary with a sigh. Far from discovering herself, the journal made her lonelier. The only person she had to talk to about these strange feelings was herself. Although she gave off an air of aloof eccentricity to others, inside she was desperate for a confidante.

It was winter 1970, and the icy weather reflected Anny's mood. Out of desperation, she accept an invite to spend Christmas in Brighton with a friend; an acquaintance really. And she didn't know any of the other people who'd be there. But there were no better offers, so she packed her bags and headed to the coast.

'Have a drink,' one of them laughed, shoving a glass of sherry into Anny's hands. She was so nervous, she gladly took the drink. It tasted sweet and sticky on her tongue, and a warmth spread into her throat. When offered more, she welcomed it.

One of the woman nonchalantly mentioned a girlfriend. Anny's heart thumped in her chest – had she really admitted that out loud? Before long, it became clear it wasn't just this one woman – all of them were gay! Half a bottle of sherry later, the word she'd been too scared to write in her journal came popping out of her mouth. 'Us lesbians…' she declared, slurring her words slightly.

'There's a meeting after Christmas,' one of the woman told her as she was leaving. 'You should come.'

'What kind of meeting?'

'Gay Liberation Front.'

'Ok,' she heard herself saying, confidence boosted by the alcohol.

A few weeks later, she stood outside the Arts Lab on Drury Lane in the cold and dark, willing herself inside. She took a deep breath, and stepped through the door. The room was poorly lit, and smelt of damp. It wasn't much warmer than out on the street. It was busy though, mainly men, smiling, kissing, chatting, some in great excitement. Many dressed strangely. Anny smoothed down her Woolworths skirt, and tightened her neatly pulled back hair. Slipping into the shadows, she found herself a seat.

From her hidden corner, Anny watched the room. There were no more than around 20 women. Are they really all lesbians? she thought to herself. Did they all sleep with other women? Did they kiss and touch each other's bodies? It didn't seem real. She watched them move around the room, greeting each other with such confidence. She felt like a wilting plant.

On one side of the room a man held a camera, which he slowly panned around. Anny's breath caught in her throat. She leaned forward, and tapped the person in front of her on the shoulder. 'Excuse me,' she said, and pointed at the camera. 'What's that all about?'

'They're making a film,' the stranger replied. 'Called Come Together.'

The camera swung round and seemed to point right at Anny. She slunk down in her chair. She wasn't ready for this level of exposure.

The meeting began. There were speeches, punctuated by clapping, whistles and whooping. Some reached such a pitch of excitement that they could only communicate by hugging and kissing. There was mention of revolution and liberation. Someone yelled: 'Fuck the family!' and people cheered. Anny wanted to disappear. She didn't feel outgoing enough for any of this. She left feeling dejected.

Anny grew up in Belgium, and developed a political consciousness as a teenager learning about the Democratic Republic of Congo (DRC). Watching them fight for independence, she questioned what she'd been told in school about civilising the Congolese. Then Algeria rose up against France; Patrice Lumumba, the Congolese independence leader and later prime minister, was murdered. Africa seemed on fire. Feeling helpless, Anny joined the Communist Party, handing out leaflets around town. Her efforts felt weak compared to the brave independence fighters.

Back then, she'd never have linked this struggle for independence with her own oppression. Yet the Gay Liberation Front (GLF) meeting made her question things about her life. She felt angry. The outside world had convinced her that she was congenitally deformed. Despite her discomfort at the meeting, she decided to go back less than a month later.

Stonewall riots

The gay liberation movement began in 1969 in New York, out of a powder keg of police harassment and civil unrest. The initial match was thrown into the The Stonewall Inn, which was popular amongst the growing gay and lesbian community, despite its overflowing toilets, no running water and drinks watered down beyond recognition. It was run by the Mafia, who passed envelopes stuffed with money to the police, in what was known as gayola. In return, they mostly left them alone. When there was a raid, the corrupt cops would tip off the owners. They'd hide the alcohol they didn't have a license to sell, and cover up any other illegal activities. Then the main lights turned on, signalling that everyone should stop touching.[2]

The thing that everyone loved about The Stonewall, was that you could party all night. There were two dance floors, which were painted black, making it very dark inside, with pulsing gel lights. At the back, queens frequented a smaller room, checking their make up in cracked compact mirrors, and teased their hair into wild styles. They received a bitter reception at every other gay bar or club, but The Stonewall welcomed them. Then there were the runaways and homeless gay youths, who shoplifted to afford the entry fee. They were too young to be let into the legitimate bars, but at The Stonewall they turned a blind eye. It became a community centre of sorts, for young gay men rendered homeless by family and institutional rejection; and for those who'd taken refuge in New York in hope of finding a place where they could be themselves.[3]

Not everyone was so enamoured. New York mayor, Robert F Wagner Jnr, was livid. In response to the number of gay men and lesbians moving to the city, he pledged a clean-up. He revoked the alcohol licenses of all the gay bars, and sent undercover police officers out to entrap as many gay men as possible. Thousands were arrested for solicitation or lewd behaviour. Some had their names published in newspapers, which meant they lost their jobs. Even clothing was policed – fewer than three pieces deemed appropriate to your gender could put you in handcuffs.

On Saturday 28th June 1969, everything changed. At 1.20am, four plain clothes policemen in dark suits and two patrol officers in uniform, arrived at The Stonewall Inn. It came as a complete surprise— nobody was tipped off this time. The lights came up, the music stopped and the police instructed people to show their IDs.[4]

Ejected patrons spilled out on to the street. At first the atmosphere was festive. There was laughing and joking; people striking poses and bowing. Someone shouted, 'gay power!'; people sang We Shall Overcome. An officer shoved a transvestite, who responded by hitting him on the head with her handbag. The crowd booed.

A lesbian in handcuffs was dragged out of the bar. She escaped repeatedly, fighting with four of the police officers, swearing and shouting. A sense of discomfort spread, as restless high spirits merged into anger. Coins were thrown, pinging against the side of the police wagons. The woman looked at the bystanders and shouted: 'Why don't you guys do something?' An officer picked her up and heaved her into the back of the wagon. The cents and quarters became stones and bottles, as the crowd became a mob.[5]

The police tried to restrain them, knocking a few people down, inciting the mob further. Rubbish bins, bottles, rocks, and bricks were hurled at buildings, breaking the windows. Tyres were slashed, and another group overturned a police van. The crowd cheered and started an impromptu kick line. Just as the line got into a full routine, the police advanced again, wielding their batons, chasing the crowd down the street.

One bystander reported: 'I just can't ever get that one sight out of my mind. The cops with the [batons] and the kick line on the other side … I think that's when I felt rage. Because people were getting smashed with bats. And for what? A kick line.'[6]

The community had taken enough. It wasn't anything any one person said; no organised demonstration; it was a critical mass moment on that particular night in that particular place.

The riots played out for around five days. The message was clear: things were changing. The oppressed were fighting back. Within weeks the GLF formed. There had been gay rights groups before, but many considered their tactics weak. The GLF took their name from the National Liberation Front, who were fighting the US in Vietnam; they took their tactics from the civil rights movements, with the ideal to restructure American society. They were the first organisation to use the word 'gay' in their title.

GLF London

Two British activists – Bob Mellor and Aubrey Walters – were hanging out in New York at the time of The Stonewall uprising. They met at the Revolutionary People's Constitutional Convention in Philadelphia, called by the Black Panthers. They returned to Britain full of big ideas and fighting spirit. On 13th October 1970, they held the first GLF London meeting at the London School of Economics Library. It was a modest beginning, with 19 people attending. But it grew rapidly, becoming a watershed moment in British queer history.

It was an era of all-round repression in Britain: the National Front was on the march; and in Notting Hill, black power activists were falsely accused of inciting a riot. But those with their backs up against the wall were fighting back: in Brixton the British Black Panthers formed; Women's Liberation activists stormed the Miss World contest at the Royal Albert Hall; and in Northern Ireland The Troubles reached their peak. The GLF found themselves in the thick of it, getting thrown out of pubs, suffering police intimidation and queer-bashing.

From the beginning, the GLF saw itself as part of a wider movement fighting exploitation and oppression. In early 1971, when the Conservative government introduced the Industrial Relations Bill – a piece of legislation designed to limit strikes – the GLF stood alongside the trade unions. Armed with placards, as well as balloons and feather boas, they joined the marches. However, the trade unions didn't take well to the tongue-in-cheek slogans, such as 'poof to the bill'. They were made to march at the back. Despite this, it was an important day for many gay people, who'd never come out publicly before. Wearing their lavender GLF badges, they chanted: 'Two, four, six, eight, gay is just as good as straight; three five, seven, nine, lesbians are mighty fine.'[7]

In 1972, the Industrial Relations Act came into force. Five dock workers defied the act and were arrested. They were sent to Pentonville Prison, and a wave of strike action began in solidarity amongst printers, miners, transport workers and others. Demonstrations took place every day outside the prison gates, which GLF members attended.[8]

As well as being class conscious, the GLF aligned itself with the women's movement. They recognised that they were both oppressed by the patriarchy. Rejecting stereotypes of men and women, they were both vilified and outcast by society. GLF members performed street theatre with Women's Liberation groups outside Bow St Court, where the Miss World activists were on trial.

Within a couple of months, Anny found a completely new life. Every week was a frantic mix of meetings; think-ins (all day meetings on a particular topic); Gay Days in local parks (a pre-cursor to Pride); and many smaller awareness groups. She went leafleting at The Gateways, London's only lesbian club, inviting the women to join the GLF. They were robustly ejected from the premises.

Women only squats

The GLF was about living your politics, as well as talking about them. That led some to explore alternative housing solutions, including communes where fixed gender roles were rejected and children were the shared responsibility of the group. This led to the development of a number of women-only communities, especially around Hackney. By 1970, there were an estimated 50 women-only households behind Broadway market, including one continuous terrace of seven women's squats.[9]

Anny became involved in the Hackney squatting scene. The collective action of changing the locks held symbolic significance to her, and there were always numerous Yale barrels and keys in circulation.

The interest in the women-only squats was practical as well as political. The 1970s saw a huge housing crisis, with people struggling to find homes while properties stood empty. The issue of housing was a particular problem within the queer community, as they were more likely to be rejected by landlords, vilified or even beaten up in their quest for a home. Squatting was a way to address the injustice, and sort the problem of having nowhere to live.

While some of the properties were in good condition, many were in a poor state of repair, needing water and electrics reconnected. Many women enrolled on evening courses or read books to develop their skills. Support groups started, including Women in Manual Trades, which still exists today. By the mid-1970s, there were a growing number of women electricians and plumbers fixing up properties to squat.[10]

It was often the local residents who told lesbians when a house was empty. They didn't want a neglected property next door as it might become overrun with rats, and contribute to the dereliction of the street. Lesbians were recognised as a group who repaired houses and got them back on their feet.

As well as a solution to the practical issue of housing, the squats provided community. They supported a growing women's music scene, and other cultural activities, such as poetry and photography groups. There were sports events, with Sunday hockey on London Fields, and some independent feminist bookshops. On Christmas Day, the women went out to paint over racist National Front slogans.[11]

Despite this women's utopia, lesbian mothers were still vulnerable to the courts. One woman lost custody of her daughter to her male ex-partner. His case focused on her living in a communal lesbian squat, as evidence of unfit parenting.[12] In 1984, Rights for Women, a London based charity fighting to improve the legal system, published The Lesbian Mother's Handbook and Lesbian Mothers on Trial.

The split

According to Anny, the enthusiasm and idealism that had been so attractive at the beginning, was also the cause of the GLF's downfall. Meetings became too big to be manageable, and too often used as an opportunity for male cruising. The women felt overwhelmed by the men, both in terms of numbers and the issues discussed. Some men accused the women of being less oppressed because their sexuality had never been legislated against; while the women felt their issues were not taken seriously.[13]

Anny got organised with the other women, and produced an issue of the GLF magazine, Come Together. The editorial read: 'We share the experiences of our gay brothers but as women we experience them differently [...] As lesbians, "women without men", we have always been the lowest of the low. Only through acting collectively can we overcome our own passivity and your male chauvinism [...] which perverts and imprisons us all.'[14]

The next move Anny described as predictable – they split from the men. The GLF continued on without the women, but became increasing fractured. By 1973, it had collapsed completely.

The Women's Liberation Movement

The Women's Liberation Movement had been going only a year when the women walked out of the GLF. In October, they attended the annual national conference, held in Skegness. It's formal platform of speeches, full of academic jargon, was a culture shock to the ex-GLF members. Many felt silenced and frustrated. When one of the lesbians grabbed the mic and announced a walk out, two-thirds of the room left.[15]

The conference came back together in the evening, but the women continued to struggle to get lesbianism on the agenda. The Chair dismissed the subject for being a personal matter. Despite this, the audience seemed open to discussing it. Finally, the issue was dragged out of the closet and into the room.

It would take three years before sexual identity was properly discussed again. In April 1974, lesbians held their own conference, attended by around 300 people. They agreed sexual orientation was central to feminism, and should no longer be sidelined. They asked for a workshop at the national conference in June, to open the debate up more widely. The workshop was agreed, but it came with a good deal of antagonism between both sides. Expressing the feelings of many lesbians at the conference, Margaret Coulson wrote: 'If the women's movement is committed to the rights of women to control their bodies, then we must be clear that this means not only the right to control our fertility but also the right to define and develop our own sexuality.'[16] It would take until 1976 before lesbianism was no longer an issue that divided the movement.

Anny's legacy

Although short lived, the GLF was instrumental in providing a pathway to self-liberation. It allowed individuals to speak the words 'lesbian' and 'gay' publicly for the first time, throwing away shame and celebrating their difference.

While women were in the minority in the movement, they made their voices heard. They were part of the group that spent months of discussion and editing to create the GLF Manifesto, which challenged their daily oppression, including in psychiatry, schools and the media. Today the GLF's legacy is seen in numerous policies and social norms: homosexuality is no longer classed as mental illness; different types of families are discussed in schools; and same sex couples dance together, without causing uproar, on Strictly Come Dancing. While it's still far from a perfect world, especially for our trans siblings, things have come a long way thanks to Anny and the GLF.

Meanwhile, through the squatting scene, Anny was part of a movement that created a lively and vibrant grassroots community. As well as raising awareness of government cuts and the housing crisis, they created a rich cultural and sporting life. They showed alternative ways of living are possible; ones that are not locked into rigid gendered and heteronormative rules, but through a shared and collaborative space.

From the 80s, squatting and ideas around communal living declined. Yet in the following decades, households across the country moved towards greater equality and the loosening of gender boundaries. While women still do far more housework than men, the disparity has decreased.[17] Without the radical ideas and actions of women like Anny, we'd undoubtably be further back than we are today.

In the last few decades, exorbitant rents and stagnating wages have triggered an interest in squatting again. The Office for National Statistics found that there are 1.4 million empty properties in the UK. Maybe its time for a new generation to pick up where women like Anny left off?

Chapter 10

Jane Rise Up!

It was 1979, at what would be the last Women's Liberation conference. Seventeen-year-old Jane Connor was attending. 'It just all went to shit really,' she remembers.[1]

That doesn't sound like a life changing moment, but for Jane it was about to become one. Because at that conference, her and a group of young women were going to shake things up.

The women's movement of the late 60s and 70s always had two different schools of thought: the socialist feminists, who believed that women's liberation must be sought in conjuncture with social and economic justice, and were prepared to make alliances with men; and radical feminists, who believed the only way to liberate women was by bringing down the patriarchy, so viewed all men as the problem. They held together through a shared consensus about abortion rights and equal pay, but by the mid 70s the schisms had grown wider.

Within the conference was a workshop for young people to express their views, which Jane attended. As young people often do, they complained about not being listened to or understood. Yet it wasn't just a moaning session. From that workshop was the spark of an idea – to create a new feminist youth magazine. So in the depths of the winter of discontent, with the Women's Liberation Movement falling apart, this group of idealistic young women brought Shocking Pink in to the world. A feminist fanzine with a neon glow that would grab everyone's attention, from the BBC to The Sun.

The feminist alternative to Jackie

Jane was born in 1962 in Tanzania in East Africa. Her parents were missionaries, from a nonconformist Protestant church. When Jane was a toddler, the family moved back to England following the end of British rule. They settled in a small village outside Bradford in West Yorkshire. Her father continued his work in the church, and her mother became a teacher in a primary school in Bradford, in the heart of the Pakistani community. With a strong aptitude for languages, her mother learnt Urdu so she could engage with families. From there she developed an interest in children with special educational needs and disabilities. That lead to the family moving to London, where Jane's mother worked to help disabled children in Barnet access mainstream education.

At the time of their move, Jane was 15. It was a culture shock coming from a small West Yorkshire town to the capital. At her school, her friends had bohemian parents who were artists, writer and actors. They were very different from her own family. It took her in a new direction, where music became a big part of her life.

It was the post-punk era with the rise of ska. Jane went to a lot of gigs at the Lyceum, Marquee and 100 Club. She remembers: 'I bought the first EP by The Specials. I was the first person in Muswell Hill to buy it. I was very proud to be ahead of the curve.'

The punk scene unleashed a DIY culture, which Jane embraced, starting her own band called Buddy Hernia and the Rickets (Jane was a Ricket). They recorded an EP, got it press and sent it to John Peel, who played it on his radio show. It was reviewed in the NME, and they played a few gigs around London. 'It was exciting,' Jane said. 'They say you get 30 seconds of fame, and that was mine. They were fab years. You had a Tory government, so things were grim, but there was an amazing counter culture going.'

Jane found inspiration in her teachers in school. One of them was Stella Dadzie, who went on to become a leading figure in the UK's black women's movement. Jane was also influenced by her local youth club. It was a girls group, which did all the usual things youth clubs do to build confidence and have fun, with a subtle bit of consciousness raising on the side. By the time she was 16, she was politically active, joining Marxist youth groups and CND. By 17 she was at that Women's Liberation conference, just as it was all going to shit.

Although that 1979 conference was the beginning of the end of 2nd wave feminism, it was far from over for the wider movement. Recruiting help from iconic feminist magazine, Spare Rib, and legendary photographer, Jo Spence, Jane and her friends started work on the first edition of Shocking Pink.

The idea for Shocking Pink was to challenge the false ideas of femininity portrayed in popular culture, showing girls and young women real images of themselves. It was born in to a harsh economic climate, and deployed a ferocious critique of politics. It covered topics such as contraception, abortion, sexuality, violence against women and girls, racism, women's rights, arts and culture.[2]

Although inspired by the punk DIY and fanzine culture, the young women had big ambitions. Jane recalls:

We were going to be a feminist alternative to Jackie. We wanted to create a popular magazine for young women by young women. It was ours. The agenda was set by a collective of women aged between 11 and 19 or 20. We met at the Cockpit Theatre in a meeting room. I remember that at one of the meetings there were sisters, who were 11 and 13, and their feminist mum had brought them. It was heady, heady days!

The first edition launched with a flurry of publicity. There was a lot of media interest. Jane was interviewed on Radio One; there was a feature in the Guardian; there was even stuff in the tabloids, although Jane remembers it as a bit patronising. It didn't come without it's controversies. 'Age was a taboo,' said Jane. 'It might have been fine for Cosmo to speak about orgasms and the clitoris, but this was girls, children really, talking about it.'

Although third wave feminism was still some years away, Shocking Pink pioneered ideas about intersectionality. Jane explains:

There was a photo story about Michelle, and her coming out story at 14. She's a working class lesbian and she comes out at school and gets bullied. It was quite challenging. We picked up on a lot of challenging issues like that: racism; class; gender and the experiences of Irish young people, in terms of The Troubles.

Jane was involved in Shocking Pink for around 18 months, before leaving to study at the University of Sussex, in Brighton. There she joined the Labour Party Young Socialists and the National Organisation of Labour Students. She found work in a wholefood restaurant, but got in trouble for dying her hair bright red and nearly lost her job. After graduating, she moved to Manchester, where a new chapter began.

The miners' strike

In Manchester, Jane threw herself into political activism full time. It was 1984, and all about the miners' strike.

The 1984–85 miners' strike was a major industrial action to prevent the closure of coal pits, that the Conservative government deemed uneconomic. The strike was led by Arthur Scargill of the National Union of Mineworkers (NUM), against the government run, National Coal Board. The strike began in Yorkshire and spread to South Wales, Scotland, North East England and Kent. Strikes took place across and the Midlands and North Wales, but there was less support in these areas. This led to high tensions and conflict in an attempt to stop miners from breaking the strike.

Four months into the strike, two men – Mike Jackson and Mark Ashton – decided to organise a bucket collection for the miners during the 1984 Pride march in London. The response was so positive they called a meeting to organise further. Lesbians and Gays Support the Miners (LGSM) was born, and within months there were groups across the country, including Manchester, Brighton, Southampton, Lothian, and one in Dublin. Most people were already active in trade unions and/or left parties, including Mark Ashton, who was general secretary at the Young Communist League. Like the GLF, they were class conscious, building the organisation around the trade union philosophy: an injury to one is an injury to all.[3]

LGSM's main goal was fundraising for the miners and their families, who were unable to claim any benefits while on strike. They went to clubs and pubs, got drunk, had a flirt and a dance, then they took a bucket outside when the night ended. The reception was mostly positive, although some asked why they weren't collecting for AIDS. Others were from the mining communities themselves, and had bad experiences there. They came to London to escape that life, so refused to contribute. Others gave gladly. As the campaign grew, miners came to London to talk to the community about their plight. In one crowded gay pub in Kings Cross, a miner stopped the music to address the crowd and received an ecstatic response.

The single biggest fundraiser was the Pits and Perverts benefit gig in London's Electric Ballroom, on 10th December 1984, where they raised £5650. Bronski Beat, featuring Jimmy Summerville, headlined and there were moving speeches by the miners or their wives and girlfriends. They were all greeted by thunderous applause and cheering.

Up in Manchester, Jane was collecting in pubs and bars. 'We organised a fundraising gig at the Hacienda," she explained. 'Tony Wilson gave the venue to us for free, and we got the Buzzcocks to headline.' In total, LGSM raised £20,000 for the miners, equivalent to over £75,000 today.

The government had sequestered the funds of the NUM, which meant any money donated directly to them would be inaccessible. So support groups adopted specific communities, delivering the money to them directly. In a clapped-out van, Jane and her friends headed to the East Lancashire coalfield they were twined with, unsure of the reception they'd receive.

In 2014, the film Pride explored the unlikely alliance between the LGBT community and the miners. In the film, when the activists first arrive there is tension, which eventually dissipates when they start to understand their shared oppression. In reality, they were warmly welcomed from the start. The miners even organised a social for them. 'I remember doing a slow dance with a woman,' Jane explains. 'Not someone from the coalfields, but from the solidarity groups. It was fine. Maybe there was an odd look, but never any hostility.'

Fellow LGSM member, Ray Goodspeed confirms this attitude: 'When we arrived in the hall, after a kind of pin drop moment, we got a round of applause. There was no question of anybody walking out.'[4]

In the documentary, All Out! Dancing in the Dulais, an un-named women from the mining community says: 'It's only over the last year that we've got to know gay and lesbian people; their struggle is something similar to ours. We've suffered in the last year with the police [...] what they've been suffering all their lives ...'

Women's groups

Still identifying with the women's cause, Jane split her time between LGSM and Women Against Pit Closures. This movement grew out of a network of local support groups, set up by women in mining communities at the start of the dispute. In May 1984, a rally in Barnsley brought many of these groups together for the first time. Two months later, they established a national coordinating committee to strengthen links between the women.

One of the key figures was Jean McCrindle, who helped set up the first support group in Barnsley. She argued that women should be encouraged to attend rallies and take an active role in the campaign. The groups consisted of mainly working-class women. Some had been politically active for years, while for others it was their first experience of activism.

Jean was well known in socialist circles, with the NUM and other trade unions. She had links with the Women's Liberation Movement, which she used to gain support from urban feminists. She organised reciprocal trips between communities, so the women could campaign together and learn from one another's perspectives. A national women's rally against pit closures took place in London on 11th August 1984. The route went from Trafalgar Square to Burgess Park in South London. As they passed Downing Street they fell silent, to express their disgust at how the government was treating their families.

Women Against Pit Closures empowered women in the coalfield communities, connecting them to women's rights and other protests, such as Greenham Common. The role of women in the strike totally reversed the NUM's attitudes, which prior to 1984 were steeped in sexism.[5]

Jane saw first-hand the power of the organisation. 'It was women leading the struggles. Women taking on the logistics exercises, and being really really well organised and great at raising money. The meetings we had were all about the women – miner's wives, aunties, daughters, supported by women from the labour network.'

Other women's groups included Lesbians Against Pit Closures, which launched in November 1984. They formed out of a frustration with LGSM, where meetings could be dominated by 'very gobby men'.[6] Others felt intimidated or bored by some of the party politics pushed by the male LGSM members. The group focused on raising money, which they donated to a women's organisation in Nottinghamshire.

The end

Thatcher was determined to crush the NUM, who she perceived as having too much power. Her strategy was to build up stocks of coal; keep as many miners at work as long as possible; and use the police to break up protests, which they often did with extreme brutally, including raiding individuals' homes. The government mounted a legal challenge against the strike. It was eventually ruled as illegal, as there had been no national ballot of NUM members. On 3rd March 1985, the strike came to an end. It's considered by many to be the longest and most bitter industrial dispute in British history.[7]

The defeat significantly weakened the NUM, and destroyed mining towns. Once vibrant communities became places of mass generational unemployment, poverty and other social problems. With the largest and most powerful union out the way, when New Labour came to power in the late 90s they swiftly placed further restrictions on the entire movement. This significantly weakened labour rights across many communities, leading to an era of stagnant wages.

Today, wage growth remains at its lowest in peacetime since the Napoleonic Wars.[8] In what seems like a prophesy, Mark Ashton said in 1984: 'The miners, and workers in general, need defence organisations, and that's what unions are. What this strike is about is the government trying to smash those defence organisations and smashing the unions. I'm not going to stand for that because if you start with that, there's no stopping it.'[9]

Although LGSM's support for the miners was always unconditional, in 1985 the NUM and mining communities of South Wales joined them on the London Pride march. That same year, the NUM supported a call for lesbian and gay equality at the Labour Party conference and TUC conference.

In 1985, LSGM folded, reforming briefly in 1992 when the government announced a new wave of pit closures. In 1987, Mark Ashton died of AIDS, aged only 26 years old. All the miners came for his funeral, with their banners and bands.

After LGSM, some of the activists got involved in the print workers strike. Others campaigned against Clause 28, a piece of legislation that prohibited the 'promotion of homosexuality by local authorities'. This in effect stopped any discussion of queer issues in schools between 1988 and 2000.

In 2016, a new group of queer young activists took up the mantle. Lesbians and Gays Support the Migrants formed to challenge the hostile environment policies of the Conservative government. They staged protests outside the Home Office, and blocked deportation flights at airports. In 2017, several members of the group were arrested and charged with terrorism.

The also targeted the founding stone of gay liberation – Pride. In 2018, they occupied British Airways' observation tower in Brighton, over the company's sponsorship of the march. They considered it pinkwashing due to their role in migrant deportations. In 2022, they organised a die-in at the event against the Met Police's involvement. The protest lasted 23 minutes, to represent the 23 people who died in police custody that year. In 2024, both generations of LGSM came together to organise the Pits and Perverts 40th anniversary party.

After the strike

In 1985, Jane returned to London and focused on her local Youth CND group.

> We had a local group in Haringey, but also marches organised nationally around US bases in the South of England. You'd march for 10–15 miles and then you'd be put up in a Quaker hall or something like that. That was brilliant fun and we were highlighting what was going on at these bases, at the same time as Greenham was going on.

The ongoing fight for social justice took its toll on Jane. The 80s was a decade of continuous struggle, and by the early 90s she was burnt out. In 1996, she had her first child and wasn't very active, other that within her trade union. For many years she worked as Director of Public Health in the London Borough of Greenwich, which saw her take a leading role in the fight against Covid in 2020. During the Jeremy Corbyn years, she rejoined the Labour Party and took a leading role in Waltham Forest Momentum. In 2021, she helped organise a Reclaim the Night march following the murder of Sarah Everard.

Jane's legacy

Jane helped trail blaze a new era of feminism, which was more inclusive of different women's lives. With LGSM, she promoted an ideology of cooperation and solidarity between different oppressed groups. As well as breaking down political and social barriers, they made different sections of the left, from trade unions to the Labour Party, more progressive places.

Jane's part in prioritising women in the movement was vitally important. Working with Women Against Pit Closures, she played a role in cementing alliances between different groups, something the early women's movement struggled to do. By providing once voiceless women with their own space, they found power to organise alongside other labour groups.

Sadly, during this era of history the most successful woman in the room was Thatcher. She succeeded in crushing the miners and wider trade union movement. In a 2002 interview, she was famously asked what her greatest achievement was. She replied: 'Tony Blair and New Labour. We forced our opponents to change their minds.'[10] In the late 90s, Labour finished the job she started with aggressive anti-trade union laws, which weakened them further. This led to the collapse of industrial communities across the UK, which have never fully recovered.

Following the miners' strike, support for trade unions dramatically declined. Since the 1980s, membership has halved.[11] There's been a small increase more recently, especially during the Covid 19 national lockdown. In 2023, the TUC claimed 90,000 more members.[12] Yet it's light years away from its heyday. Employment practices in companies like Uber make it harder for workers to organise, while Amazon have a sustained campaign of union busting. This has had a dramatic effect both on wages and stability of work, with zero hours contracts and fire-and-rehire practices widespread.

Jane's generation saw injustices of race, gender, class, sexuality and disability as a catalyst for collective action. The collapse of the trade union movement put a boot in the gut of solidarity movements. Identity politics moved into the space left. Rather than fighting to change institutions, the movement seeks better representation within the systems that oppresses them. As Lesbians and Gays Support the Migrants show, this often leads to pinkwashing and other corporate marketing spin. We forget the stories of women like Jane at our peril.

Chapter 11

Olive Rise Up!

A poster was stuck to the wall of the Sheffield theatre venue declaring, Black Liberation Week. An image of Huey Newton, founder of the US Black Panther Party, shone out from the middle. He was holding a sub machine gun.

On the door, a short, slightly stocky woman with a loud voice was handing out programmes, and directing people to their seats. As Michael approached he felt drawn to her. 'Have one of these,' she said, in a strong South London accent, shoving a programme into his hands. 'And you can sit over there.' He smiled back, shyly.

It was 1970 and Michael was a lecturer at Sheffield University. He'd become interested in the Socialist and Anti-Imperialist Society, who were organising that evening's event. The woman on the door was Olive Morris. Already pulled towards her energy, Michael struck up a conversation after the event. She explained that they wanted to bring some black speakers up from London. Michael offered to go in the van to help organise things. It was so packed, she had to sit on his lap. From that awkward journey, their relationship grew.[1]

Olive was born in Jamaica on 26th June 1952. She lived with her maternal grandmother and five siblings after her parents, Doris and Vincent, migrated to Britain in search of better work. Vincent found a job as a fork-lift truck driver, and Doris in a factory. In 1961, they brought Olive and her siblings over to South London. Life wasn't easy. Olive had a difficult relationship with her father, and spent time in care during her childhood. She frequently moved between schools, where she experienced persistent racism. At 16 she left, with no qualifications.

In 1969, she abruptly entered politics when she intervened in the arrest of a Nigerian diplomat, Clement Gomwalk. The diplomat had parked his Mercedes to go shopping with his family at a popular record shop on Atlantic Road in Brixton. Under their stop and search powers, the police questioned him, believing the car was stolen. They didn't believe he was a diplomat, and according to witnesses, dragged Gomwalk from behind the wheel and proceeded to beat him. During his brutalisation, a crowd gathered and police reinforcements were called. Legend goes that Olive burst through the crowd, and demanded they let the man go. However, she later said she didn't arrive until after police had taken Gomwalk away. She was arrested trying to defend a friend, whose arm had been broken by a police officer. She was thrown to the floor, racially abused and beaten, before being taken to the station.

While in custody, the police claimed not to believe she was a woman, due to the androgynous way she dressed. They made her take her jumper and bra off to prove she was female. Then they threatened to rape her. Her brother Basil said she was barely recognisable she was so badly beaten. She was fined £10 (over £1300 today) and given a three month suspended sentence.[2]

It's said this incident catapulted her into activism. She became interested in the Black Panther Party, and in 1972, advertised in Time Out for a travel companion to Algeria. She hoped to visit the US Black Panther Party leader, Eldridge Cleaver, who was living there in exile. Nobody answered her advert, so her friend, Liz Obi, offered to join her.

They left Dover on 7th August 1972, and travelled on the overnight ferry to Calais. They hitchhiked through France, where they faced a lot of hostility. In Spain, people seemed less bothered by the sight of two young, black, female hitchhikers. They took a ferry from there to Morocco, and intended to continue travelling on to Algeria, but ran out of money. They had to go to the British Embassy and ask their parents to wire them some so they could return home.[3]

Despite this early misadventure, Olive remained determined. With Liz, she joined the British Black Panther Movement. The group was unaffiliated with the Black Panther Party in the US, but they had the same basic principles – to serve the black community. This included running

Saturday schools to combat racial discrimination in education. Olive took on a leadership role in what was otherwise a male dominated movement.

During the 70s, there were a number of court cases with black people on trumped up charges. This includes the Mangrove Nine trial, which the British Black Panthers organised a picket at each day. The nine were accused of trying to incite a riot after organising a protest march against police harassment at The Mangrove, a Caribbean restaurant in Notting Hill. The activists were found not guilty, with the judge acknowledging the police's racial bias.

Outside the court there were skirmishes, and Olive was arrested with two others. They were charged with assault. At the trial, they took a political stance, asking for members of the jury to be black, working class or both. They researched the judge and found out that he'd prosecuted participants in the anti-colonial Mau Mau Uprising in Kenya. During the trial itself, the nine witness police officers gave contradictory evidence. The jury acquitted Olive and the other defendants.[4]

In 1973, the British Black Panthers disbanded, and Olive established the Brixton Black Women's Group with other women from the British Black Panthers. It was the first black women's group in Britain, and allowed them to organise with feminist issues front and centre. They helped connect, educate and empower black women in South London, set up a journal called Speak Out, and created the Black Women's Centre.[5]

Trade unionism

Olive was active in the trade union movement, including visiting the picket lines at Grunwick in 1976. Grunwick was a film processing factory in Willesden, with a large migrant workforce, mainly Ugandan and Kenyan Asia women. The conditions in the factory were reminiscent of a Victorian sweatshop, with long hours and low pay. Overtime was compulsory, often with no prior notice; and the women had to ask permission from male supervisors if they needed the toilet. The factory owners refused union recognition, so the women felt they had no choice but to put up with it.

On 20th August 1976, Devish Bhundia was dismissed for working too slowly. Five other workers walked out in solidarity. The six started picketing outside the factory to show their anger and frustration. Gradually others joined. The factory responded by sacking them all.

Word spread, and workers from other industries joined the picket. By November, 8000 were on the streets in protest, making it the largest industrial action since the General Strike in 1926. The police were called, and violence erupted. By the end of the day, 234 people were injured and 550 arrested.[6]

The strike received widespread media coverage, and the workers were dubbed the 'strikers in saris' due to their ethnicity. It attracted widespread support from the white trade union community. It was an anomaly, however. In general, the main trade unions continued to ignore the needs of the black and Asian communities. Eventually Olive grew tired of the internalised racism within the labour movement, saying: 'On countless occasions we've found that the movement does one thing for white workers and another for black workers. White workers have time and time again refused to give our unions recognition, they have crossed our picket lines for racist reasons, they have organised against our organisations.'[7]

Self help

Brixton faced a particularly intense housing crisis, due to severe property shortages. The existing stock was in a state of deterioration, and nobody was building to rent. A mix of economic and discrimination issues made finding property especially hard for people in the Caribbean community.

Olive saw housing as a human right, and squatting as a direct action to secure that right. In 1973, she moved into a flat above a shop at 121 Railton Road in Brixton, with Liz Obi.

Unlike with council properties, squatting privately owned buildings could be challenging. The owners and property agents waged war against squatters, aided by the police. Olive and Liz were arrested several times, but simply came back to the property after each release.

One of the most notorious incidents was on a cold January morning in 1973. While Olive was at work, the police forcefully removed Liz and brought her to the station. When Olive returned, they were waiting for her. She climbed onto the roof and shouted down at them. According to Michael, she threatened to jump if they didn't leave her alone. In one of the most famous pictures of Olive, which made it onto the cover of the Squatters Handbook 1979 edition, she's angrily pointing a finger in the property agent's face. Behind them a sign says: 'Legal warning. This property has been occupied by squatters. We intend to stay here. If you try to evict us, we will prosecute. You must deal with us through the courts.'

That's eventually what they did. Through endless legal wrangling, they made it hard for the women to stay in the property. So they moved down the road to squat a council property at 64 Railton Road.[8] This became the home of Sabaar Bookshop, which specialised in black women's literature.

Olive was very tidy, taking pride in her home. She didn't always have the tools of a housewife, so would scoop up dirt and dust with a folded newspaper. It was sparsely furnished, with a sofa and casa pupo rug from Spain, bought for her by Michael. He sanded the floors for her too. She covered the walls in political posters, and there was always some music on. It was mostly reggae, but never Bob Marley, who she felt wrote too much to the tastes of white people. According to Michael, she preferred 'more rootsy people' like Nicky Thomas.

In the evenings, her and Michael took turns cooking, and went down to the off-licence to buy a quarter bottle of whiskey between them. Afterwards, they'd sit in front of the TV, Michael on the sofa, Olive on the floor between his legs. 'It wasn't just politics.' Michael explained.[9]

Squatting wasn't traditionally a black movement, and was dominated by white activists. This didn't bother Olive. Michael remembers:

She was the least sectarian person I knew. She would work with anybody, so long as they were genuine about what they were doing. There was a defensive tendency within the black movement, with some saying they wouldn't work with any white people. Olive was very open to all people. You saw this in her daily behaviour. She would talk to anybody on the street. It used to take us sometimes half an hour to walk from Brixton tube station to her flat on Railton Road because there were so many people she had to stop and talk to. There would be old people, young people, black people, white people. It didn't matter. As soon as people talked to her they felt that warmth and commitment.[10]

Life in Manchester

Olive embraced lessons from any source, and frequently treated older friends as mentors. Yet she felt her academic disadvantage keenly. So in 1975, she moved to Manchester to study for a degree in social sciences. She devoured every academic text, and took extra studies in maths and French to reclaim the education she'd missed out on. At lunchtime, she sat in the cafe planning political activities, including with Black Women's Mutual Aid and the Manchester Black Women's Co-op, which aimed to support the needs of young mothers in Moss Side. She got involved in anti-apartheid and anti-immigration campaigns, and fought against the government's proposed tuition fee increase for overseas students. The charge didn't affect her directly, but she saw it as a racist denial by Britain towards its former colonies, who looked towards the motherland for opportunities.[11]

Olive was an internationalist, and worked with the National Co-ordinating Committee of Overseas Students. In 1978, she visited China, which deeply impacted her. She felt there was a lot to learn from their model of self-help and self-reliance, and was eager to share this new found knowledge on her return. Despite all these extra curricular activities, she graduated in 1978 with a 2:1.

Olive's relationship with Michael was fluid – they both had other romantic partners during their time together. While Olive was in Manchester, she had a relationship with a woman. In the many articles written about her, virtually none mention her sexuality. It's not even mentioned in relation to her squatting in Railton Road, which had a well established queer community, similar to that of London Fields in

East London. It's unlikely to be a coincidence that she settled on that particular street.

In an oral history interview with Michael, he seems hesitant to discuss it, although he mentions that her sexual identity raised questions at the time. This was possibly because of the gender non-conforming way in which she dressed, in t-shirt with Black Panther badges, jeans, small afro and either bare-foot or in comfortable shoes. It's been described as a 'queer revolutionary sister soul look'.[12] The term soul sister is linked to soul power; a melting pot of black nationalist political strategies, with black cultural consciousness, including a celebration of black music, fashion and culinary traditions.

After Manchester

After completing her degree, Olive move back to London. She found work at Brixton Community Law Centre. With Michael, she wrote a pamphlet called, Has the Anti-Nazi League got it right on racism? It questioned whether the Anti-Nazi League was right to fight fascism when there was so much institutional racism. Olive was exasperated by the failure of white-led progressive groups to see where battles needed to be fought. She argued that the National Front was merely a symptom, and not the cause of racist ideologies, which were built into the fabric of society. She urged people to stay focused on where racism affected daily life, such as in schools, the police, local government and even trade unions.[13] Meanwhile, with Stella Dadzie and ex-Panther comrade, Beverley Bryan, Olive set up the Organisation of Women of African and Asian Descent. It held its first conference in Brixton.[14]

Cut short

In 1978, Olive and Michael went on a cycling trip in Spain. They'd been training in London, to ensure they were fit enough to take on the adventure. But one day they were cycling up a moderate hill and Olive stopped. 'I can't do it,' she said to Michael.

'It's not very steep. Just lower the gears,' he replied.

'I can't do it. My legs just won't do it, and my back's aching.'

Eventually it became clear she couldn't continue. The trip was cut short, and they returned to London.[15]

Back home, her health deteriorated. Her friend, Gerlin Bean, recalls the day when they were hanging out at her house, laughing and having a good time. Suddenly, Olive bent double in pain. At first, Gerlin thought she was messing around, but after realising how ill she was, she called a taxi to King's College Hospital. There, Olive experienced what has now become a well documented form of institutional racism – the downplaying of black women's medical needs. According to Gerlin, they told her it was gas, and sent her away with some medication. The pain didn't go away. Eventually she was diagnosed with non-Hodgkin lymphoma.[16]

Olive approached her illness with the same level of righteous anger as she did everything else. Judith Lockhart, who met Olive through the Brixton Black Women's Group, remembers how angry she was at the possibility of her life ending so early. Judith said: 'She'd lost a lot of weight and she came out of bed and she was, I think, walking back out with us [...] and she just kept saying, 'I don't want to die ... I'm too young to die' [...]She wanted to make one last trip.'[17]

The cancer treatment was not successful. On 12th July 1979 she died. She was only 26 years old. Hundreds of people came to her funeral, and many more to the memorial a week later. The Brixton Black Women's Group published an obituary in the third issue of its newsletter, praising Olive for her 'total dedication to the struggle for liberation, democracy and socialism.'[18]

Olive's legacy

Following the 1985 Brixton riots, Lambeth Council named their new building on Brixton Hill after Olive, following a campaign by the Brixton Black Women's Group. The building housed the council tax and housing benefit office. Five years later, it had been outsourced to Capita. Residents were evicted for non-payment of rent because it took Capita over three months to process housing claims. Liz Obi said: 'Those of us who remembered Olive would often remark that she must be turning in her grave to know what was being done to the most disadvantaged members of the community in her name.'[19] If she was still alive she would've organised a demonstration against Capita outside the building.

Despite this recognition, when surveyed in 2007, few people in Brixton knew who she was. Several confused her with the black British-Jamaican nurse Mary Seacole, who lived over a century before. Others thought she must've been a councillor, as her name appears on a municipal building. So the Do You Remember Olive Morris? community art project was launched to bring attention to her short but impactful life. The project included events, talks, film screenings and radio shows.

In 2008, the Remember Olive Collective (ROC) formed to create a more permanent archive to her life and increase public awareness. In 2021, a blue plaque was unveiled on Talma Road in Brixton, where she once lived.

Less than 30 years after it was built, Lambeth Council announced the closure and demolition of Olive Morris House. In April 2020, a protest was organised to save it. It was unsuccessful. ROC are currently fighting for a foundation stone, with inscription, for the site.

Olive was a tireless fighter for social justice and equality, and packed an enormous amount into her 26 years. Politics was not something she went into for self-advancement, but for the good of the community and its people. Her story should inspire today's young people in what is possible, regardless of your background. In an era of increased hopelessness and disengagement from politics, we must keep Olive's story alive.

One way the ROC work towards this is through the Olive Morris Memorial Awards. Created to remember Olive's radical grassroots activism, they celebrate a new generation of young women and non binary activists of African and Asian descent.[20]

Society often struggles to hold the name of more than one black woman in its collective consciousness, hence the confusion with Mary Seacole. The work of the ROC is vitally important to protect Olive's legacy, and make space for more than one black female hero.

Part IV

1990–2020

Chapter 12

Julie Rise Up!

A young Asian woman stood on Bethnal Green Road in Whitechapel. Small, with dark hair, she wore a cardigan, with a long scarf wrapped around her neck, like a Bengali Dr Who. She watched the young, brown-skinned men, with placards and loud voices. Yelling back were skinheads, bodies covered in angry, blue tattoos, and hatred twisting up their faces. Police officers with riot shields edged forward, plastic visors and helmets pulled down low. Some were on horseback, as they had been 60 years earlier at the Battle of Cable Street. Like then, the young activists knew the police weren't there to protect them.

A group of police officers emerged from a van with large dogs. As the yelling increased, the dogs strained on their leashes, barking at the protestors. The Asian woman pushed her way through the crowds. A comrade joined her, and they positioned themselves in-between the activists and the police. They stood peacefully, in defiance, protecting the men.

Several decade later, Julie Begum recalls: 'We knew that they would go after the young men, so we got in front of them to stop that. We knew it would have been harder for them to put their dogs on [young women]. Obviously it doesn't stop them but we knew the men were an easier target.'[1]

It was not Julie's first stand-off with aggressive dogs. The eldest of three siblings, she'd protected her younger brothers on the way home from school. They'd had to go past a dry-cleaners that had a large German Shepherd. The dog would be set on them for no reason other than to cause fear. Julie explained:

In a way, [the protest] was a recurrence of that experience. Even when I was younger somehow I knew that I'd be able to protect my younger brothers. I suppose I felt righteous anger at being attacked, and feeling that because it was wrong we'd be protected somehow. It's more of an emotional thing than anything based on any rational thinking. I couldn't not get involved and not say something. To remain silent and stand by, it's just not a part of my nature.

Julie was born in Mile End Hospital in June 1968, into what had become an increasingly tumultuous world. In April, Martin Luther King was assassinated in the US; in May, France narrowly avoided a civil war after students in Paris rioted; Ford sewing machinists in Dagenham held their landmark strike for equal pay; and opposition to the Vietnam War reached its peak around the globe. While far away from these world changing events, Julie's life in Tower Hamlets reflected the growing global tensions.

The melting pot of migration

The modern London Borough of Tower Hamlets was formed in 1965, merging the districts of Bethnal Green, Popular and Stepney. It gets its name from the proximity these boroughs have to Tower Bridge, and its historical village-like status beyond the city walls. Over centuries, many different groups of immigrants settled in these hamlets.

In the sixteenth and seventeenth century, the Protestant Huguenots fled France, following persecution from the Catholic church. Many ended up in the East End. They were artisans, especially weavers, and helped move Britain from an agricultural society into an industrial one. In Spitalfields they left behind their footprints in places like Princelet Street and Fournier Street, with grand houses financed by a booming silk weaving trade.

During the 1840s, the Irish came in their hundreds of thousands. Although they'd been coming for centuries, the potato famine caused an influx, as they fled starvation. The 1841 census lists 289,404 Irish born people in London; by 1851 this figure had nearly doubled. The majority of that population lived in the East End.[2]

By now, artisan crafts were in decline, replaced by sweated trades as a less skilled, impoverished population was willing to work for lower rates. This included in tailoring, shoe making and on the docks.

Next it was the Jews, whose stories we've explored in previous chapters. The growth of the railways provided opportunities to move to greener areas, with more spacious housing, for those who could afford it. In their place came migrants from the Asian sub continent, particularly Bangladesh. With it emerged a new era of racial tension.

Up until the 70s, the Bengali community in Britain consisted primarily of men in low paid jobs, who lived in shared accommodation. Like Julie's father, they were often from low socio-economic backgrounds, uneducated, and often illiterate. Julie's grandfather had died when her father was only 10 years old, forcing him into a job at a rickshaw workshop to make ends meet. In 1966, he took the opportunity to migrate to Britain, as part of a voucher scheme to attract immigrants from Commonwealth countries. He found work as a machinist in Jewish and Turkish textile factories, which were in their dying days. He sent a big chunk of his meagre earnings back home, so his siblings could get an education.

Then the British government changed the immigration laws, shutting the door on Bangladesh and other Commonwealth countries they had previously courted. Fearing permanent separation from their families, many moved their wives and children over to Britain. Julie's father was still unmarried, but decided he should find a wife while he could. He married a girl from his home town in Bangladesh – the eldest daughter of a local family. She was a teenager, and also illiterate, having spent most of her life caring for her younger siblings. She found herself thousands of miles from home, in a country where she didn't speak the language or know the customs. Yet with a determination she'd pass down to her daughter, she made friendships with other migrants from around the world. This included an Irish neighbour, who would sometimes walk Julie and her siblings to school so they could stay safe.

The housing crisis

Due to institutional racism, it was difficult for most migrant families to qualify for council properties. Those who'd left recession hit northern towns for the capital were accused by local authorities of making themselves intentionally homeless'.[3] Julie's family were one of the lucky ones. They secured a one bedroomed council house on an estate in Spitalfields, for five of them. Like many migrant families, Julie lived on a predominantly white estate, where they were victims of intimidation and violence.

Julie remembers how tough life was as a child in Stepney in the 70s:

> There was a lot of unemployment and social unrest. Not a pleasant time for anyone, but particularly for migrants of black or Asian origin. There was high levels of racial attacks and violence that permeated in all areas of our lives: in our housing, education, services, and even the police. There was a climate of hostility that was always around. You knew you weren't wanted and weren't really accepted. Most people kept a very low profile; just tried to get on without being attacked or harassed on a daily basis.

Julie remembers one family on their estate where they lived, who were a particular menace. When Julie was eight years old, one of their sons made her eat dog faeces because 'he thought that was the kind of thing I ate.'[4] Julie ran home to tell her parents, and her father came out and challenged the family. The situation escalated, and the police were called. Despite this family being already well known to the authorities, they arrested Julie's father.

The Bengali community have a long history of community activism, and easily carried this into the East End. While squatting was predominantly a white movement, Asian families occupied empty properties in Spitalfields and Whitechapel, to provide safer housing for their families. By the mid 70s, the number of Asian families squatting had reached into the hundreds. In Spring 1976, around 50 Asian families already in squatted accommodation formed the Bengali Housing Action Group (BHAG).[5] It was supported by the Race Today Collective, a magazine by leading figures in the radical black movement, including the British Black Panthers.

A leading figure in the BHAG was Mala Sen. Mala was born into a military family in northern Indian in 1947. When she was 15, she met and fell in love with Farrukh Dhondy, and the couple eloped to Britain in 1965. They both began writing for Race Today, and Mala organised a mass demonstration against racism in Birmingham, which was attended by over 2000 people. Mala believed that supporting people to claim their rights was the best way to achieve political change. She said: 'When you are a political activist, you empower other people to take a chance to empower themselves.'[6]

It was within this spirit she worked with the BHAG, helping families open up empty buildings. At the height of the squatting movement, a property on Woodseer Street in Spitalfields had 200 families living in it.[7] BHAG set up vigilante patrols to defend against eviction, and racist attacks. This included by the state, who cut their gas supplies, and the National Front, who smeared excrement on doors and firebombed properties.

The BHAG continued to liaise with local government, advocating for the community's rights. Overrun by the sheer number of squatters, in 1977 the Greater London Council (GLC) announced an amnesty, granting all squatters the chance to register and secure a formal tenancy. The BHAG drew up a map defining a safe living area for the Bengali community, which the GLC accepted. This established Brick Lane as the Bangladeshi heartland of Britain.

Mala's role within the BHAG was 'crucial especially when it came to building work or dealing with the authorities or the media.'[8] In an interview with BBC Radio 4 in 2015, Farrukh said: 'She was a leading light in the East End.' Yet she was far from the only South Asian woman making her mark. Although Bengali women either didn't work, or worked from home, and weren't encouraged to have a public life in the same way as women from other cultures, they played an important role in the fight for housing.

Historian, John Marriott said: 'Far from the view that women are passive victims of religiously based male oppression, Bangladeshi mothers are determinedly matriarchal, exercising firm control over their families. Women attended to the needs of their families and were determined to keep them, their homes and themselves safe from racism.'[9]

Housing campaigner, Charlie Forman echoes these views. He commented: 'It has been women who have been the most militant about staying in the Spitalfields area. They stand to lose more than their men, and have frequently dissuaded the men from signing for distant flats even when there is apparently no other choice.'[10]

Altab Ali's murder

Despite these huge victories in housing, the community was still far from safe. Growing up in the area during that time, Julie remembers:

> There were lots of no-go areas in Tower Hamlets for Bengalis. Even Brick Lane could be very hostile. There was a clear delineation where the railway bridge is, where it cuts across, where there's one side with more Bengali restaurants and businesses and the other side wasn't so much. People knew if they went beyond, towards Bethnal Green, they might get their heads kicked in. This did happen on a regular basis. Growing up in Globe Town where I did there was high levels of hostility. There was other places in Bow, Isle of Dogs, Poplar, that were just disgusting.

On 4th May 1978, Altab Ali, a Bangladeshi textile worker, was stabbed to death in a random, racially motivated attack. On his way home from work in Brick Lane, he was left in a pool of blood on Whitechapel Road, after three teenagers attacked him. He was declared dead on arrival at the Royal London Hospital.

Altab Ali's death came a year before Margaret Thatcher came to power. Police brutality and institutional racism was rampant, with hate crimes rarely prosecuted. Police often dismissed requests for protection. They sometimes took part in the violence itself when the community protested against discrimination. Thatcher blew that dog whistle even harder, when she said: 'People are really rather afraid that this country might be swamped by people with a different culture.' A year after these words were televised, she became Prime Minister.[11]

Julie was only 10 years old at the time of the murder, and her parents tried to shield her. But she remembers hearing her cousins and uncles talk about it:

> There'd been murders before, but this particular murder generated a lot of activism. Thousands of Bengalis and non-Bengalis got together to organise protests and demonstrations. There was a demonstration to Downing Street with Altab Ali's coffin, via Hyde Park. That was the beginning of organised resistance in terms of Bengali youth movements and young men realising they weren't going to accept this kind of treatment any more. The generation before turned the other cheek, trying to not resist. The younger men were much more angry. They found it unacceptable.

A number of youth movements formed, uniting with other anti-racist and anti-fascist groups under the umbrella of the Asian Youth Movement (AYM). They were influenced by other radical solidarity movements, both in the UK and US. They would confront racists on the streets when they were trying to smash up Bengali shop fronts. Others set up cultural projects, like community centres. There were demonstrations and a march from Whitechapel to Whitehall, under the slogan: 'Here to stay, here to fight.'[12]

By the early 80s, some from the AYM moved into mainstream politics, becoming councillors in Tower Hamlets. Julie explains: 'There's been lots of progress made in the way that the Bengali community have been working collectively to empower themselves. That has resulted in certain gains in mainstream politics, as well as local politics. The Bengalis were one of the first groups to became active in local government.'

Self discovery

Through the 80s, tensions in Tower Hamlets increased. Julie struggled her way through secondary school, which she described as 'like being in prison.'[13] There were fights in the corridors, a pupil took an overdose in the toilets, pupils assaulted teachers, and bullying was rampant. At that time, boys came out of school and went to prison, and girls ended up having babies.

Yet Julie knew this was not the life for her. She did well in school, got some A Levels, and secured a place in a teacher training college. The course was not always easy, and she nearly dropped out after experiencing racism and inequality on one of her teaching placements. One of her college lecturers gave her a talking to, encouraging her not to quit. She listened, and qualified, and got a teaching job at Tower Hamlets College.

After a few years, the college forced new terms and conditions on its staff, and Julie realised she didn't want to spend the rest of her life teaching. Still in her 20s, she decided to go on an adventure. She joined Voluntary Services Overseas, and was sent to Nepal to train their teachers in skills other than rote learning. On returning to London, she taught basic literacy and computing skills to refugees and asylum seekers in Bethnal Green. Later she joined the Museum of Childhood, and then the Geffrye Museum (now the Museum of the Home) collecting oral histories from those growing up in the East End. Yet this era of self discovery was about to be rudely interrupted.

The rise of the BNP

In 1993, the resignation of a Labour councillor in Tower Hamlets triggered a by-election. The British National Party (BNP) put forward a candidate – Derek Beackon – under the campaign banner, 'rights for whites'. He focused on canvassing and leafletting, rather than large public meetings, which would often get disrupted by anti-racist organisations. The campaign was a success, with Beackon gaining the seat from Labour by seven votes. He became the BNP's first elected councillor.[14]

The BNP victory triggered widespread condemnation across the country, including from the Archbishop of Canterbury, George Carey, and Met Police Commissioner, Sir Paul Condon. The Daily Mirror ran an article with the headline: "Sieg Heil ... and Now He's a British Councillor." Staff and other councillors at Tower Hamlets staged a protest walk-out after his election, refusing to work with him.

It wasn't just smart campaigning that led to the BNP victory – they also used intimidation tactics. Many local Asians were terrified of voting, because racists came into the borough from other areas, and assaulted people on their way to the polling stations. When Beackon's seat came up for re-election in 1994, Julie knew it was time to mobilise.

Women Unite Against Racism

Julie was part of a generation of women who'd been brought up in England, and were literate, articulate and wanted to make their voices heard. Yet there was frustration amongst many of the women, who felt excluded from the anti-racist and anti-fascist movement. Julie explained: 'There was always the same men at the same meetings making the same statements. As women, we decided we wanted to do it differently. We wanted to make meetings accessible for women and girls to attend.'

When they organised a conference to see if there was a mandate for that kind of organising, hundreds turned up. Julie continued:

We decided that we would do it in a collective way, having a rotation of people speaking at meetings. It wouldn't be this cult of leadership that was often seen at lots of different events. We made sure that meetings had childcare support or provision. We wanted to connect with women that would not normally engage with political activism, finding out what was important for them, what they wanted to say about what was going on in their lives. We worked collaboratively with different faith groups, trade unionists, anti-racist movements. We were also from diverse backgrounds ourselves: black, white, Asian, other backgrounds.

Taking inspiration from the black civil rights movement in the US, the women started by registering people to vote. They made sure information was available in a variety of languages, including Somali, Bengali, Chinese and more. They came together in each other's homes and made banners and posters, and organised demonstrations every week in the run up to the elections. Knowing that the threat of violence was keeping people away from the polling booths, they established escorts to support other women in casting their vote.

In May 1994, the votes were in. In a nod to the voter registration campaign by Women Unite Against Racism, turn out rose from 44% to 66%. Beackon lost his seat to the Labour Party. Julie describes the moment of their victory: 'Beackon was defeated and our job was done. It was amazing. It was euphoric. We realised that we'd achieved what we wanted to do in a way that was really going to have a positive result for everyone in the borough. There was a sense of jubilation that really was amazing.'

Julie's legacy

After the election victory, Women Unite Against racism disbanded. They had set out with a mission, and achieved what they wanted to do. As usual, history books do not always recognise their contributions, but the figures on voter turn-out speak for themselves.

Women Unite Against Racism challenged stereotypes about Asian women, and changed the lives of individuals involved. Julie explains:

> It was a very important time of our lives where we felt empowered to do something, but on our own terms. I think it changed us all in many ways and left a really important legacy. It showed that it is possible to do things differently; we don't have to do things the way they've always been done by other people. We need to question existing structures and organisations around how they represent experiences, so they're not just a cliché of what an activist is.

Ending the campaign at that point was essential to Julie. 'It was important to say, great, we achieved what we wanted. We didn't need to carry on. It was non-stop really for that year. It took over our lives and that intensity is very difficult to maintain. We had other things we want to do with our lives.'

Riots by white supremacists across the UK in August 2024 shows that racism is still very present in our society today. Julie reflects on how the political landscape has changed:

We've gone from being Pakis to terrorists. That has had a huge implication, not just locally but internationally. The perception of Muslims really is something that is much bigger than what was around 30 years ago. Back then it was mostly the colour of your skin. Now it's not just your skin, it's your religion that is a threat to people. It's intensified a kind of discrimination against groups of people that has never been seen before.

Today, Julie is Chair of the Swadhinata Trust, a secular community group that works to promote Bengali history and heritage amongst young people. Operating since 2000, they run seminars, workshops, exhibitions and create educational materials for young people across the UK. The organisation is putting this proud and important heritage alongside mainstream narratives, so all communities have a history they can look back on. Julie explains:

I think it's really important to recognise the contributions and impact immigrants have made to a particular neighbourhood. Because we're from that neighbourhood we wanted to make sure that was recognised. It goes back hundreds of years. We've got Huguenots and Jews and Irish and Bengalis who've been making this place what it is for centuries.

Spitalfields has changed beyond measure since Julie was a child. The brick tenements replaced by glass and steel, of what the Save Brick Lane campaign calls 'a tsunami of soulless corporate developments.'[15] They now fight against a proposed shopping mall in what was once Bangladeshi heartlands. While their campaign has mobilised thousands of people through online petitions and email campaigns, Julie argues that the days of migrant grassroots activism are over in Tower Hamlets.

> There will never be another wave of migrants like the Bengalis. Because London is simply not affordable to people like that any more. Since Margaret Thatcher introduced Right To Buy, people have been buying up social housing and renting it out in ways that are not affordable for working people. It's very difficult to get fair rent for property in London any more. It'll never be the same.

Yet the struggles remain, which is why Julie's work to record the history of this defiant community remains vital.

Chapter 13

Sonali Rise Up!

Smoke poured on to the dance floor, and hands shot into the air as the drum roll broke, a new tune crashing onto the crowd. They erupted in cheers, some spontaneously hugging each other. Sonali watched from beside the DJ booth, as gurning faces grinned at her. She didn't know any of them but smiled back anyway, shifting the camera and tripod to her other shoulder. There was a tap on her arm, and a security guard pointed to a door at the back of the room. She nodded, picked up the rest of her equipment and followed.

The room was full of gorgeous looking nameless people, surrounding Irvin Welsh and Annie Nightingale. She awkwardly pushed through the crowd. 'Hi,' she said, and the two celebrities looked at her blankly. 'I'm Sonali.' She gave them her biggest smile, but they still looked vacant. Irvin was swaying slightly from side to side, as he took another swig of beer. 'I'm the documentary film maker,' she explained, feeling a bit of a fraud. She was a first-year media arts student, doing a favour for her older sister. 'I'm with the Free Satpal Ram campaign,' she continued. Her celebrity interviewees finally broken into a smile. 'Oh yeah, right,' Irvin gushed. 'Come in, come in. Where do you want us?'

'[Annie Nightingale and Irvin Welsh] were both very supportive of Satpal's case,' Sonali remembers over two decades later. 'But they were both very worse for wear. We were talking about Satpal, and suddenly Irvin jumped up and said: "I'm going to perform a new piece I've just written." Then he launched into this narrative poem. The way people showed support could be quite …quite unusual.'[1]

Who is Satpal Ram?

On a November evening in 1986, twenty-year-old Satpal Ram strode down the dark streets of Birmingham. He pulled his coat collars close around his neck to keep out the cold, his two friends joking and laughing beside him. They reached the Sky Blue Indian Restaurant. As they opened the door, the warmth and rich smells of cumin, coriander and garlic, enclosed long fingers around them, pulling the friends inside.

While Satpal's mouth watered in anticipation of his food, he didn't fail to notice the group of six white people on the other side of the room. Their table was littered with empty beer bottles, their red faces hard and tight. Satpal exchanged quick looks with his friends, as racist abuse streamed out of their mouths.

'What the fuck is this fucking music?' one of them yelled at the waiters.

Satpal fidgeted on his crushed velvet seat. Fuck this, he thought. 'Oi brother!' he said to the waiter 'Turn up the music.'

The room went quiet as all eyes turned on him. Then the man with the reddest face grabbed a beer bottle, smashed it on the edge of the table, and lunged at Satpal.

Satpal still had a penknife from work in his pocket, and reached for it as the man landed on him. They wrestled together, and when they came apart there was blood everywhere. People were yelling and screaming as Satpal checked his body. The blood was not coming from him.

Satpal later learnt that the man's name was Stuart Pearce. He was rushed to hospital, but was too drunk and aggressive to receive treatment. He later died of his injuries. A week later Satpal turned himself into the police, who charged him with murder.

Prior to his trial, Satpal had only 40 minutes with is barrister, Douglas Draycott QC. Later in an interview with The Guardian, Satpal said: 'I've never refuted that a man died as a result of my actions […] I accept that loss of life is wrong, but if I hadn't done what I did I would be dead now.'[2]

Satpal argued that in the context of a racially divided Birmingham of the 80s, where attacks on Asians were commonplace, his actions should be seen as self-defence. Draycott told him that due to the number of wounds Pearce sustained – six in total – this plea was destined to fail. Yet he had misread the pathologist's report. Although there were six wounds, only two of them had come from a knife blade. The rest were superficial, and a result of rolling around on broken glass.[3]

Events further conspired against Satpal when he reached the courtroom. Asian witnesses, who could've supported Satpal's version of events, were not called. One who did make it to the stand was dismissed because his English wasn't good enough. No translators were employed. At one point the Judge said he would translate even though he didn't speak Bengali. Satpal described the hearing as 'a complete farce'.[4]

Unsurprisingly, Satpal was found guilty and given a life sentence for the fatal stabbing of Stuart Pearce. Draycott wrongly told him that he didn't have grounds for appeal. Satpal was left to draft the application himself, in which he cited the failure to provide interpreters for the witnesses. He secured two appeals. Both times the judge ruled that failings by the defence were not good enough grounds to quash a conviction.[5]

Three years after Satpal's sentencing, his friends and family began campaigning for his release. It was picked up by wider grassroots activists, who could see the injustice in Satpal's conviction. This included Sonali's older sister, who soon pulled her on board too.

Growing up outsiders

Sonali's parents were migrants from West Bengal, near Calcutta, moving to Leicester in the 60s. The city had a sizeable migrant population but it was predominantly Gujarati and Punjabi. As Bengalis they were in the minority. 'We didn't benefit from the texture or fabric of a sizeable migrant community,' Sonali explained. 'I probably knew every Bengali in Leicester, and they have been round my mum and dad's house and had a meal. I think it's fair to say the whole family felt they had an outsider status.'[6]

Sonali's father was a lecturer at Leicester University, and her mother a social worker. Both experienced racism at work, although it was more visceral for her mother who worked on the frontline. Sonali experienced racism at school, describing the teachers as 'quite vocally racist and violent'.

These experiences destroyed her confidence, and left her managing a lot of anxiety as she internalised the racism.

Yet Bengali culture has strong roots in left politics and the arts. Unlike other families, discussions about socialism and communism were commonplace in Sonali's family. She drew confidence from it, developing strong ideologies. 'Politics was where I found the confidence that was missing on a personal level,' she explained.[7]

Initially however, there was little space in which her desire to change the world would fit. As a teenager, she was concerned with the environment; about acid rain and CFCs. There were no environmental activism groups in Leicester however. She made do with membership to Friends of the Earth, DIY poster making, and talking to anyone who would listen.

There was also little community activism for her to tap into, being one of the few Bengali families in the area. Yet this social isolation drew them closer as a family. She developed particularly strong bonds with her sister, who she describes as an inspiration. Her sister had a long history in activism, following in her father's footsteps through the trade union movement. Later she got involved in campaigns against police brutality and deaths in custody, which naturally led her to the Free Satpal campaign. When she encouraged Sonali to join, there was little hesitation.

Free Satpal Ram

By now, Sonali had moved to London and was attending demos with her sister, handing out leaflets and helping with local press work. Then the campaign went in a new, innovative direction, with the activists organising within the music scene. They approached the British Asian band, Asian Dub Foundation, asking if they could have a stall at their gig. It was low key, with an audience that was already familiar with Satpal's case. Then Asian Dub Foundation secured the support slot on the Primal Scream tour. This allowed them to break through, bringing their music to a wider, white audience. The Free Satpal Campaign came with them, with a stall at every gig on the tour. In 1997, Asian Dub Foundation released the single, Free Satpal Ram, featuring Primal Scream.

Soon there were campaign stalls at gigs and clubs around London and Birmingham. As part of the stall, they had a mass petition. Sonali loved bands, clubs, dressing up and going out dancing, so she felt right at home in this environment. She'd roamed the club asking for petition signatures. She worked out that queues for the toilets and cloakrooms were the best places to target people, getting them when they couldn't move.

'People were off their faces. Really very drunk and worse for wear,' Sonali explained. 'But we would be having these conversations not just about Satpal, but the wider criminal justice system and the nature of systemic racism. We got a lot of support from people who probably would have never thought about it before.'[8]

Yet others had. In 1994, the Criminal Justice Bill was going through parliament. Described as clamping down on anti-social behaviours, the bill targeted raves and free parties, especially on the traveller festival circulate, which were growing in popularity. The bill became infamous for containing the clause 'any gathering of 20 or more people where "music" includes sounds wholly or predominantly characterised by the emissions of a success of repetitive beats'. Author, Joe Savage, criticised the bill for making judgements about people's lifestyles, while cultural studies professor, Jeremy Gilbert, claimed it was a direct attack on people from alternative cultures. It was the first and only time a youth culture was legislated against.[9]

'I feel that there was overlap between that and the Satpal Ram campaign,' Sonali explains. 'Suddenly there was a politicisation of people who normally wouldn't have been politicised because their way of life was being legislated against. Some of those people I was haranguing with my clipboard were learning how to organise themselves in a different arena. There was definitely something in the air.'[10]

Meanwhile in prison, Satpal was trying to survive what he called 'endemic racism'.[11] He experienced beatings; was threatened with hanging; endured a total of four years in solitary confinement; and lived out his time trying to avoid becoming yet another death in custody statistic. 'They would come in and shout at me calling me racist names. Seventeen-stone men would shout "you black c***" at me.'[12]

Awareness raising by the Free Satpal Ram campaign, and others like Amnesty International, had an impact on his conditions in prison. Things eased off when the guards realised the media spotlight was on them.

After 10 years in prison, Satpal was eligible for parole. This was finally granted in 2000. However, Home Secretary, Jack Straw, over-ruled the decision because Satpal refused to admit guilt. Satpal may have stayed in prison, if a month earlier the European Court of Human Rights had not ruled on another convicted murder. They said politicians couldn't over-turn the decisions of a parole board.[13]

In June 2002, Satpal was eventually released, to much jubilation from the campaigners. But he left prison into a crazed, celebrity fuelled world. After years inside, with significant and sustained trauma, he needed to be with friends and family. Instead, he was seduced into a world of glamour and hedonism. Tensions grew between the grassroots activists, many of whom were his friends, and the world of celebrity.

'When you're trying to resolve a miscarriage of justice you don't really think about what it's like for that person.' said Sonali. 'It's all about the win. And you so rarely get a win. I know the first few years after his release the worry about Satpal didn't really go away.'[14]

The Iraq War

When the Iraq war began, Sonali was working at a dot com company, which she described as 'an a-political place full of very right-wing people who thought they were very liberal'. An email went round the office, which purported to be from an Afghan woman, who was facing horrendous treatment in Afghanistan. Sonali wondered why it had been sent out of the blue, from a company who usually didn't involve itself in international affairs. It was just before the invasion of Afghanistan, and Sonali describes the email as 'pseudo feminist cover' for military action.[15]

Disquieted by events in the Middle East, Sonali joined the Stop the War Coalition. While she saw her sister at every demo, this marked a period of more independence from the family, and finding her own political voice. Although her opposition to the Iraq war was rooted in the anti-imperialism that she'd grown up with. 'I had a visceral response to the idea of another occupation,' Sonali explained. 'I remember thinking, there can't be any more occupations, because we haven't even resolved any of the other occupations, so there can't be another one. It was a bit naive really.'[16]

Now living in Brixton, Sonali took on a more formal role with her local Stop the War branch. She also joined the Palestine Solidarity Campaign, becoming local secretary, a position she held for many years. Developing her political education, she learn to organise meetings, street stalls and broaden support through events like pub quizzes, film screenings and gigs. She'd moved from being a participant to a central organiser.

Sonali found it easy to talk to people about politics, but some of the Palestinian Solidarity street campaigning could be challenging. The group routinely faced harassment and abuse.

Loads of people involved in Palestine Solidarity are Jewish, but there weren't many Palestinians in our group. Maybe one or two British Palestinians and the rest were lefty Jewish people, who were very committed and had been organising around Palestine for years. As a brown person, I felt like I was often at the brunt of any intimidation and harassment. All the conspiracy theories ... I was told I was an agent for Iran. In Brixton there is an evangelical Christian community as well and we were told we were defying God's work. With public facing work you will always get intimidation and harassment, but [with Palestine Solidarity] it was quite pointed[17]

By contrast, campaigning against the Iraq war was easier, as there was much more public support. Several polls and surveys found that as many as one in five members of the British public disagreed with UK involvement in the Iraq and Afghanistan wars. There was evidence of cynicism, especially in relation to Iraq. Many believed the 'war-for-oil' narrative carried by some mainstream media, and shared a mistrust in the government following the exposure of the 'dodgy dossier' around Iraq's possession of weapons of mass destruction.[18]

The Corbyn years

In 2015, Jeremy Corbyn became leader of the Labour Party. The following year, The Chilcot Enquiry delivered it damning verdict on former Prime Minister, Tony Blair, and his decision to commit British troops to the US-led invasion of Iraq. Blair was accused of failing to exhaust peaceful options before the invasion; exaggerated the threat posed by Saddam Hussein; British intelligence agencies produced 'flawed information'; the military were ill-equipped for the task; there was inadequate post war planning; the UK didn't achieve its objectives in Iraq; and not enough was done to minimise the deaths of civilians.[19] Following publication of the report, Jeremy Corbyn apologised on behalf of the Labour Party for its role in the war, to the families of military servicemen and women who lost loved ones, Iraqi citizens, and war veterans. In a speech in Westminster he said: 'I apologise to them for the decisions taken by our then government that led this country into a disastrous war.'[20]

Inspired by Corbyn's 'different kind of politics', hundreds of thousands of grassroots activists joined the Labour Party. Sonali was ahead of the curve, having signed up a year before under Ed Milliband. Horrified by what she described as 'throwing migrants under a bus', Sonali believed 'people like me should be in the Labour Party' to try and put the brakes on these disastrous policies. Under Corbyn, the party became a different place, and she stepped up her involvement.

Now living in Walthamstow in East London, Sonali was elected on to the executive committee of her local branch, and became a leading figure in Momentum, the campaigning group set up to support Jeremy Corbyn. Using lessons learned from the anti-war and anti-colonial movements, she mobilised volunteers to knock on doors for both the 2017 and 2019 elections.

'Under Corbyn was the first time I had even a remote belief in parliamentary politics,' Sonali explains. 'Even then it felt very precarious. Nothing was ever going to change without a grassroots movement to support him. That's where things change.'

Following Corbyn's defeat in 2019, and the election of Sir Kier Starmer as Labour leader the following year, Sonali grew disillusioned. She left the party, returning to grassroots organising. 'I feel like the British left has far too much focus on parliamentary politics and it is a real distraction,' she said. 'I think it can be an obstacle for change.'

Today Sonali continues her fight for the liberation of the Palestinian people, and against racist immigration legislation and the hostile environment. Politics feeds her career too. In 2015, she was selected from over 1,300 applicants for the Old Vic 12, a programme for developing theatre artists. She has gone on to write for radio, TV and theatre. All her work has political themes, including around immigration, capitalism and a re-imaging of The Jungle Book, with a thoroughly modern and decolonised Mowgli.

Just before the COVID 19 pandemic hit, Sonali began work on a new play called Liberation Squares. It follows the story of three teenage British Muslim girls, as they come under observation through the government's Prevent strategy. Prevent was introduced in 2003 by the Labour government, with an aim 'to stop people becoming terrorists'. The strategy disproportionately targets Muslims.

In an interview with Amnesty International, Sonali said: 'No one was really talking about Prevent, but I knew that it was having an enormous impact on people [...] Young people are being made to feel like they've done something wrong. They're not sure what they've done and they're often not sure who says they've done something wrong.'[21]

Sonali's legacy

Sonali's belief in solidarity movements has been a running theme throughout her activism. The merging of club culture, with grassroots anti-racist campaigns, was an innovative and powerful strategy, that led to the release of Satpal Ram. Themes of solidarity run through her work around Palestinian liberation too, working together with leftist Jews and others from the Muslim community.

While the perceived failure of the Stop the War Coalition to prevent further military action crushed many anti-war activists, for Sonali it was a moment of coming together. With so many joining the march in

London, she felt proud to be British, which she claims 'doesn't happen very often.' People were united and she could feel the change in public mood. 'I remember thinking, there seems to be an understanding of what it means [...] my sense of pride comes from resistance amongst British people. That's what makes me feel hopeful.'[22]

Like the generations before her, Sonali knows that we are strongest when we work together; when people, often from diverse backgrounds, join up against a shared oppression.

Chapter 13

Ziggy Rise Up

As four-year-old Ziggy stepped on to Mozambique soil for the first time, in neighbouring South African, Nelson Mandela was fast becoming one of the most famous names in the world. It was not by chance this was happening. It was part of a highly orchestrated, and arguably one of the most successful, mass civil rights mobilisations ever. Little Ziggy of course knew little about this at the time, but her parents did. They were part of a growing international movement supporting the African National Congress (ANC), a political organisation advocating for the rights of black South Africans.

South Africa had been colonised for centuries, first by the Dutch and then by the British, who wanted access to the enormous reserves of gold and diamonds buried under the earth. There were bloody, territorial wars, leaving most of South Africans under British rule. Land was moved out of the hands of the majority black citizens, who were also barred from voting.

In 1918, in a small village in South Africa's Cape Province, Rolihlah Mandela was born. When he started school he was given the English name, Nelson. In 1941, he ran away to Johannesburg to become a lawyer. There he met leaders of the liberation movement, who opened his eyes up to a world he had never seen before. He started to understand the impact of racial prejudice, unlearn his own internalised racism, and joined the ANC.[1]

In 1948, apartheid was introduced, dictating every part of life for black South Africans. They were forced from their homes and made to live in either urban townships or rural areas, which were overcrowded and impoverished. Life was completely segregated, and any person of colour needed a passport to travel into the exclusively white areas. Faced with this escalating racism, Mandela and other young members formed the ANC Youth League. They began a campaign of civil disobedience, deliberately walking into white areas without permission.

Yet the atmosphere in South Africa darken further. In 1960, police opened fire on a peaceful protest in the township of Sharpsville, killing 69 people. Most were shot in the back as they ran away. Known as the Sharpsville Massacre, it became a pivotal moment in the anti-apartheid movement. A state of emergency was declared across South Africa, and a number of black liberation organisations were banned. This included the ANC, who were forced to operate from nearby countries. While the ANC had always been a non-violent organisation, Mandela realised this wasn't going to overturn apartheid. He formed a military wing of the ANC, publishing a controversial manifesto, declaring they had to 'submit or fight'. Unlike Gandhi, Mandela saw non-violence as a tactic, not a way of life. He didn't think the tactic was working anymore.[2]

The South African government named him their 'number one terrorist', and the US placed him on their terrorism list. He was arrested, and placed on trial for treason and sabotage, for which he faced the death sentence. Mandela declared it was a cause on which he was prepared to die, but on 11 June 1964, he was instead given a life sentence. He was transported to Robin Island, a maximum-security prison.[3]

Mandela may have disappeared into obscurity if it wasn't for a new generation of student activists, influenced by the black power movement in the US. Resistance grew in the 80s, with workers mobilising through their unions. Still in exile, the ANC realised that Mandela's story could be what they needed to engage the rest of the world. The Free Mandela movement was born.[4]

Over in Britain, the South African Boycott Movement was established in 1959. Following the Sharpsville Massacre, it was renamed the Anti-Apartheid Movement. During the 80s, they worked in close cooperation with the ANC, to personalise the fight. A number of streets and buildings were named after Mandela, and several UK cities granted him Freedom of the City. In 1984, The Special AKA released Free Nelson Mandela, which reached number nine in the UK music charts. In June 1988, a special tribute concert was held at Wembley Stadium in celebration of

Mandela's 70th birthday, It was broadcast to 60 countries around the world, and featured some of the biggest stars of the day, including Tracey Chapman, Whitney Houston, Sting, and the Bee Gees. Meanwhile, the boycott of South African goods spread through trade unions, universities and into the general public.[5]

In 1990, Nelson Mandela was finally released. Having been so cut off from the rest of the world, he was taken aback by the huge crowds who came to greet him, including 'so many whites amongst them.' A new era in South Africa had begun. In 1994, Mandela was sworn in as South Africa's first black president.[6]

Back in London

This was the backdrop to Ziggy's childhood in Africa, but by the time Mandela was out of prison she'd returned to London. Initially life was tough, as she adjusted back to British culture. When adolescence hit, things got wild, with parties and a search for independence. Growing up in such a political family, with the politically charged environment in Africa, led Ziggy and her older sister to join Youth CND. It was the height of the ban the bomb movement, with women at Greenham wrestling in the road with police. It was the first time Ziggy took political action separate from her parents, volunteering at Tufnell Park Youth CND, and at the national office.

As a teenager, Ziggy continued to find London life pressured. She felt she had to show a tough exterior and be streetwise to get by. At 19 she moved to Brighton and found a new life of 'hippies and students and drumming circles on the beach.' She also found a new revolutionary politics, joining the Socialist Workers' Party (SWP). After the collapse of apartheid in South Africa, and the fall of the Berlin wall, being part of a generation that could dismantle the whole capitalist system seemed possible. But it didn't take long before she became disillusioned with the SWP, angry at their hierarchical structures and poor gender politics. Plus she still wanted to go out and party.[7]

Throwing herself head first in to the rave scene, Ziggy went to some of the big M25 raves that typified the era, but mainly a lot of free parties on the beach and in squats. There was a lot of drugs, weekend long festivals on hallucinogens, and a general feeling that the whole town was their carnival. Compared to the SWP, it was a joyful world, and although not directly anti-capitalist, there was a self-organising ethos that drew on the political ideologies Ziggy aspired to. She would often delight in repeating the (misattributed) quote from the anarchist, Emma Goldman: 'If I can't dance I don't want to be part of your revolution.'[8] In 1996, Ziggy joined Reclaim the Streets, taking this ideology and dropping it on the M41 link road in Shepherds Bush in glorious technicolour.

Reclaim the Streets

Reclaim the Streets formed in London in 1991. It emerged during a period of mass road building, which had begun two years earlier under the Thatcher government. She'd boasted it would be the 'biggest road building programme since the Romans.'[9] In total, a ten-year scheme promised 2,700 miles of new or improved road networks, at a cost of £23 billion.

Reclaim the Streets began by protesting motor shows and creating their own cycle lanes after Lambeth Council in South London refused to install them. Then word came of a major piece of road building in North East London. A link road that would connect the M11, but wipe out communities in Leytonstone and Wanstead in the process. Since 1990, the Department of Transport had been repossessing and demolishing houses. In total, around 350 houses were destroyed, along with trees and green spaces, wiping out entire communities. By 1994, Claremont Road in Leytonstone was the last street standing.

The first time the bailiffs came, there were only about 30 protestors, who gathered with their banners. The bailiffs turned around immediately. A cheer went up, and a local journalist captured the moment for the press. But they knew this was not the end; they would be back. So the protestors built their camp, taking inspiration from the women of

Greenham Common a decade before. Rather than building in a field, they built on the street. The activists dug secret tunnels, built rooftop towers, treehouses and an underground bunker. Artists turned abandoned cars into artworks, created outdoor sculptures out of waste materials, and painted houses vivid colours. They created a cafe; allotment; an intricate system of treetop walkways; pulleys to move food and water up and down from the roof tops; and shopping trolleys filled with concrete to act as road blocks.[10]

This was the year of the Criminal Justice Act, which saw the government legislate against youth culture for the first time in history. Politicised by the removal of their freedom to self-expression, many ravers joined the environmentalists on Claremont Road. Along with them came hunt saboteurs, also affected by the Act; people from wealthier parts of the borough; and homeless people seeking community and a safe place to sleep. Their camp swelled to hundreds.

It wasn't just young people. One of the last residents to remain on Claremont Road was Dolly Watson, who was 92 years old. She'd been born in her house, and lived there all her life. All she got was a letter from the Department of Transport telling her to leave. She refused. Despite all the chaos going on around her, Dolly passionately defended the activists, declaring: 'They're not dirty hippy squatters, they're the grandchildren I never had.'

Another long time resident who refused to leave was Old Mick, a tough East End character who'd barricaded his house, and showed others how to do the same. He was full of ideas and philosophies. He could see how the movement was coming together, predicting it would grow. He didn't know how right he was.[11]

Volunteers had been monitoring police compounds for signs of activity for a while. On 27th November 1994, the call came that Claremont Road was 'going to be taken'. Seven hundred police officers and bailiffs turned up in riot gear, as a DJ up in a tower played Music for the Jilted Generation by the Prodigy.

Police and bailiffs brought mechanical diggers, cherry pickers, ladders, hammers and crowbars, as every activist made themselves as difficult as possible to remove. People barricaded themselves behind corrugated iron and tyres; drilled holes in to the road, into which they sunk lock-on bolts; and attached their bodies to the towers with bicycle D-locks. The evictions went on through the night, where the temperature dropped dramatically. Most did not have warm clothes, let alone sleeping bags. In what became known as the Battle of Claremont Road, it took the authorities nearly three days and £1 million to dig all the activists out.[12]

Although the M11 link road went ahead, it raised the profile of the campaign and moral argument against road building. It also grew the movement, with many eager for their next action.

A core group of activists from the Claremonth Road protest, gathered a short while later at the Rainbow Centre, a squatted church in North London. Amongst a rabble of dogs and children colouring-in on the floor, they asked: what do we do now?

They agreed to contact their mailing list of over a thousand people, asking them to join a road block on Camden High Street. They would recreate Claremont Road there, with a sound system powered by bicycles, a cafe, and a climbing frame for children in the middle of the street. On 14th May 1995, around 500 turned up, with people dancing in the streets, blocking traffic with a party that went on all night. With the wheels now turning, occupations in Islington, Kings Cross and Birmingham appeared later that summer.[13,14]

In July 1996, it was the turn of Shepherd's Bush. Ziggy had been at the SWP annual conference that same day, attending a couple of Marxist meetings in the morning. 'It was blah blah … men talking about stuff,' she explained. At midday she went off to the Reclaim the Streets event. She said:

It was just joy itself. We took over all six lanes of the flyover motorway [...] in both directions. It's very scary when you first go on to the road, because the traffic is still moving. But it was just so brilliantly organised from the DIY culture. There were sound systems, and these figures in huge ball gown dresses on stilts walking around. It looked like just a carnival costume, but underneath they had these pneumatic drills, and were drilling up the tarmac [...] And we built this little sandpit in the middle of the road for the kids [...] It was theatrical, and a sense of the absurd [...] a lot of humour [...] and a great sense of togetherness and power to really change things. In contrast to the hierarchical organisations [like the SWP] where you get a weekly missive from headquarters telling you what your duties for the week were, it felt so free and liberating [...] After that there was no going back for me.[15]

Momentum around Reclaim the Streets grew, with actions taking place throughout the summer and into the autumn of 1996. In Birmingham, Liverpool, Sheffield, Oxford and Cambridge, activists took over roads. By 1998, the movement had spread around the world with actions in Sydney, Berlin, New York, Amsterdam and more. There were also occupations in support of Liverpool's sacked dockers and striking tube workers. In 1999, the movement reached its crescendo with the Carnival Against Capitalism.[16]

Carnival Against Capitalism

On 18th June 1999, thousands of people took to the streets of London under the slogan: Our Resistance is as Transnational as Capital. Although essentially an anti-capitalist protest, there were a variety of groups, including labour rights, environmental, feminist, animal rights and anarchists. The event coincided with the 25th G8 summit in Cologne, which brought together the eight largest high-income countries. It was part of a global day of action focused on financial districts in 40 countries around the world. Ziggy explained: 'London was one of the most powerful, in the sense that we really did take over the city. We started at Liverpool Street Station [...] and we did these [very slow] car crash things to block the streets. We stormed the Futures Exchange Building, and we set off fire hydrants.[17]

In total, around 5000 people invaded the International Financial Futures Exchange, which is part of the London Stock Exchange. They sprayed graffiti messages on the walls, disabled CCTV cameras, and played drum and bass on their sound system. While the demonstration was largely peaceful, according to the BBC, some protestors threw stones and bottles at the police. Forty-two people were arrested, and in the House of Commons, Home Secretary, Jack Straw condemned the 'deplorable outbreak of public disorder and violence.'[18]

Other peaceful demonstrations continued outside the financial districts. Three hundred cyclists disrupted traffic by riding slowly through the city centre carrying banners; the Campaign Against the Arms Trade closed down Lloyds Bank with a 'die-in'; The Association of Autonomous Astronauts, a worldwide network of community groups dedicated to building their own spaceships, formed a blockade of the arms manufacturer, Lockheed Martin; and there was a virtual sit-in of the Mexican embassy in solidarity with the Zapatista Army of National Liberation. Around 30,000 copies of a spoof version of the Evening Standard, renamed the Evading Standards, was distributed across the capital.[19]

'There was a sense of great triumph and great power about it,' Ziggy explained. 'My friend wrote later that it was the one time she felt truly ungovernable […]Which is why it was so surprising to find out later that the cops were involved in the planning.'[20]

Spy Cops

For more than four decades, British police ran a spying operation on thousands of activists. In total, 140 undercover officers infiltrated more than a 1000 political groups, compiling confidential files on their activities. Bob Lambert, one of the key figures in the surveillance, admitted '…we were part of a "black operation", that absolutely no one knew about and only the police had actually agreed was okay.'[21]

Overtime, the secrecy around the operation began to crumble due to the efforts of activists and investigative journalists. In 2015, Home Secretary, Theresa May was forced to announce a public inquiry. After a series of delays, the inquiry started hearing evidence in summer 2020.

The evidence revealed that the covert operations dated back to 1968, a tumultuous year across Europe when students and workers took to the streets. This includes the women machinists at Ford Dagenham, who were fighting for equal pay. It exposed elaborate police tactics, including developing fake personas by using the identities of dead children. During their deployment, undercover officers pretended to be activists, while feeding back information about the protestors' plans and movements to their superiors. More than 20 of the undercover officers had sexual relationships with women, who had no idea they were spies. Some even had children with them. One of these women described the revelations as being 'raped by the state', becoming deeply traumatised after discovering her partner's identity.[22] In 2010, these women grouped together and successfully took legal action against the police.

The police were forced to admit they spied on at least 18 grieving families who were campaigning for justice. This included the parents of Stephen Lawrence, who at the time were trying to get a proper investigation into the racist killing of their son.[23]

'A lot of my friends had [unknowingly] slept with policemen,' Ziggy explained. 'It's really, really heartbreaking. Having these [court transcripts] in front of us and going through it has been really painful for some of us.'[24]

Decline of the movement

Like many, Ziggy felt that the Carnival Against Capitalism failed to develop a clear strategy. So she moved to Germany and got involved in some 'more serious Marxist stuff'. After Germany, she travelled around Europe in a van with her then partner, eventually settling on an anti-capitalist commune in Northern Spain. It was part of the People's Global Action Network, a worldwide collaboration of radical, grassroots campaigns, and direct actions in resistance to capitalism and for environmental justice. The idea was to have a permanent space to develop their political activism beyond short term campaigns or 'spectacular events'. They wanted to move towards the construction of sustainable alternatives to capitalist systems, and show that a different world was possible.[25]

They settled in an old farmhouse, in a little mountain hamlet. It had once been a thriving industrial region, known for shipbuilding and mining, with strong trade union presence. As industries folded, it became run-down, with mass unemployment. But a strong left presence still lived on in popular memory. It was the perfect place to experiment with 'long term alternatives that reduce our dependency on both the market and the state.'[26]

The farmhouse was owned by a local foundation, and they leased it collectively. They called it Escanda, which is the name of a local wheat, and stood for Espacio Social Colectivo para la Autogestión, la Diversidad y la Autonomia' (Collective Social Space for Self-Organisation, Diversity and Autonomy). They ran seminars on gender and activism, a conference about the Israel-Palestine conflict, and held workshops on sustainability, gender and globalisation in a local school. They critiqued the concept of the nuclear family, exploring radical new ways of living, collectivising childcare, household chores and food production. These everyday tasks became part of their political activity.

Despite these forward-thinking ideologies, many years later, Ziggy reflected: 'It didn't really work out [...] the limits became clear, the culture changed, and I had kids.'

Ziggy wasn't the only one to move on. Without a clearly communicated vision of what it wanted, the anti-capitalist movement faded away in the early 2000s. Reclaim the Streets morphed into other things, including Guerilla Gardening and street parties against the arms trade.

Back to Brighton

Now a parent, Ziggy moved back to Brighton and life took a new turn. She found the babies linked her in with real people far more than the anti-capitalist movement ever did. She explained:

> You go to the GP a lot more, you go to nurseries, you go to baby drop-ins, to breastfeeding drop-ins. Brighton was still an alternative scene, so my mother group there was still quite hippy-baby-sling-wearing

kind of thing. But then they start primary school and you're suddenly mixing with everybody. And then I decided to train as a midwife.[27]

Ziggy describes this sudden change in direction as 'an epiphany [...] a calling or whatever'. After completing her studies, she got a job in the NHS, where she felt much more rooted in reality. Both the women she was working with, and her colleagues, were from all walks of life, and from all around the world. It was a stark change from the bubble of the anti-capitalist movement. While she still went to the Anarchist Book Fair, took her daughter to the 2017 Women's March in London, and went back to Escanda for their summer holidays, her daily life was rooted in the local community.

Today, Ziggy's work and political life have merged. She's been involved with Patients Not Passports, which advocates for people being charged for, or denied, NHS care because of their immigration status. Through her midwifery, she works with groups promoting birth choice, and has written about race in maternity care. Overall, she describes herself as becoming 'increasingly feminist'. She explains:

Even if men have good ideas and things, they're bloody annoying. They don't do the childcare, they organise meetings between 7–9pm when women can't go because they're busy, they talk over you. I love my world now because my work is all women [...] most of my political stuff is now women [...] I live in a world of women [...] I think for so many lefty women [having kids] is the first time you realise how sexist the world is.[28]

Ziggy's legacy

Having grown up watching the collapse of apartheid, Ziggy came of age thinking that anything was possible. It felt that they were on a cliff's edge, with life about to go one way or another. Looking back, Ziggy can see that the revolution was never really going to happen.

> It was good to feel the power and have all that media coverage. But
> [the movement] alienated people as well. It was a little bit privileged
> – young people that could do all that. Once you have kids you realise
> none of that would be open to single mums; it wouldn't have included
> people with disabilities; it was pretty much for cool young people
> with enough means to be able to take those kinds of risks. There
> are only certain people who can do that.

Despite its shortcomings, the movement was not without its wins. The
Conservative government's plan was to build 600 roads. By the time they
left office only 150 were built, failing utterly in their bid to be anything
like the Romans. When the Labour government came into power in
1997, they scrapped the remainder of the road building programme,
committing to an integrated transport system[29]. It's clear that Reclaim
the Streets succeeded in shifting the political narrative, getting road
expansion put on hold.

Despite the horrendous state abuse of the women in the movement,
they did rise up and win. Not only was the Spy Cops operation exposed,
but legal cases won against them.

It's hard to say whether the Carnival Against Capitalism achieved its
aims, as they were never clearly defined. Despite this, nine years later
another group of young people mobilised against capitalism. Motivated
by the 2008 financial crash, the Occupy movement organised protests
in over 951 cities, across 82 countries around the world. They operated
under the slogan: 'We are the 99%.'[30]

Arguably, the Occupy movement did shift the debate. Following their
actions, left wing populist movements emerged across Europe, including
Podemos in Spain, Syriza in Greece, and the election of Jeremy Corbyn as
leader of the Labour Party in the UK. Meanwhile in the US, a movement
emerged around Senator Bernie Sanders, who narrowly missed becoming
the Democratic Party's nominated candidate in the 2016 presidential
elections. Carnival Against Capitalism was arguably a stepping stone to
these wider campaigns.

Many of these movements have since dissipated. The question now is: what comes next? Since the Covid 19 pandemic, the ten richest men in the world doubled their fortune, while the incomes of the 99% fell.[31] Each year, rents continue to spiral way above the rate of inflation, while shanty town structures grow around the capital as increasing numbers become homeless. In 2024, The Trussell Trust distributed more than 3.1 million food parcels, including to 1.1 million children. They have seen a 94% increase in demand for support over the past five years.[32] According to the Office for National Statistics, there are more than five million unpaid carers in England and Wales. The majority of them are women, who find themselves increasingly sandwiched in-between caring for elderly parents, and their children or grandchildren. More than three quarters (79%) feel stressed or anxious, with over half feeling depressed and lonely.[33] Young people are not fairing much better, with one in five having a probable mental health disorder.[34] Rather than seeing the growing number of disability benefits claimants as a public health red flag, in 2025 the Labour Party purposed £5 billion worth of welfare cuts. It's anticipated that three million families will lose out from these proposed changes. This has drawn condemnation from a wide range of charities, activists and community leaders.

The fallacy of neo-liberalism is clear – today our lives are defined by insecurity, inequality and disintegrating communities. As Ash Sakar questions in her book, Minority Rule: 'The silent question, for lots of people, is "why are things like this?" In previous centuries, enough people asking that out loud might result in an uprising. Instead, we in the Global North are curiously deadened.'[35] If things are so bleak, why have we lost the revolutionary spirit that was so strong in the generations before?

Chapter 14

Faiza Rise Up!

'Terrorist sympathiser!' the two middle aged men shouted at Faiza. It was a freezing cold evening in December 2019, and it hadn't stopped raining all day. It wasn't that typical British drizzle either, but a proper downpour, which made it impossible to stay dry. Faiza tried to remain strong under her umbrella, smiling for the cameras.

'You can't win' the gammon-faced men said, stalking towards her.

Faiza's heart beat hard, as adrenalin surged through her. As the men drew closer, her body took over and she ran inside the polling station.

Outside, the men continued to yell as polling officials called the police. 'It felt like a bad omen,' said Faiza.[1]

Faiza was the Labour Party candidate for Chingford and Woodford Green in North East London. A relative newbie on the political scene, her charisma and authentic politics drew huge support. Street canvassing and rallies brought in crowds of hundreds; with a conveyer belt of celebrities and high-profile figures, including Hugh Grant, David Schneider, and the journalist Owen Jones. A number of leading members of the Labour Party came too, including Leader of the Opposition, Jeremy Corbyn, who picked Chingford, and Faiza, as the platform to launch Labour's 2019 election campaign.

Faiza was up against the incumbent Conservative, Iain Duncan Smith. He'd been in the seat for 27 years. Before that it was held by Tory behemoths, Winston Churchill and Norman Tebbit. But Duncan Smith's treatment of vulnerable claimants while Secretary of State for Work and Pensions, left him deeply unpopular. As well as implementing brutal cuts to benefits, he changed the eligibility criteria for sick and disabled people, making it harder to claim. In 2013, food poverty charities criticised him for refusing to meet to discuss the ever-increasing demand on their services.[2]

In 2015, the DWP (Department for Work and Pensions) admitted to publishing fake testimonies of claimants happy with their benefit cuts.[3] Later that year, new statistics showed thousands of people had died soon after being found fit to work in disability tests. Jeremy Corbyn called on him to step down. There were angry scenes when he visited a job centre in Peckham, with demonstrators shouting 'murderer!' Cancer charities joined the chorus, saying sufferers could be left homeless due to cuts in sickness benefits.[4]

A series of internal enquiries into the deaths of people claiming benefits revealed that ministers were repeatedly warned about the risks the cuts posed. While the report stopped short of directly linking claimants deaths with problems claiming benefits, it highlighted widespread flaws in the handling of claims by people with mental illness and learning disabilities.[5] That same year, Iain Duncan Smith resigned from his post as Work and Pensions Secretary, apparently in protest at the government's plans to make even further cuts.[6]

Despite all this scandal, Chingford and Woodford Green voted Iain Duncan Smith back in at the 2017 election. He would feel the bite however, with his majority slashed from 12,963 in 2010, to just 2,438.[7] Part of this was undoubtably anger at the Government's austerity policies, but the demographics of Chingford and Woodford Green were also changing. People were moving into the area from the neighbouring constituency of Walthamstow. They brought with them more liberal politics. When the Labour Party selected Faiza as their candidate, it was with a huge buzz. Could she take the seat from this Tory dinosaur?

When Boris Johnson called a winter election in 2019, many speculated it was, at least in part, to stop volunteers mobilising for Labour. It didn't work. Thousands turned out on the streets, mostly from Momentum, a grassroots organisation set up following Jeremy Corbyn's leadership election victory. In Chingford and Woodford Green, they broke records for the number of doors knocked; at rallies people chanted Faiza's name; people stopped her in the street to hug her, cry, and one woman even bought her flowers. On the day Hugh Grant turned up, a local baker made them a cake 'as if it was an engagement party.'[8]. Online the campaign blew up too, with rap legend Stormzy retweeting Faiza's campaign video. Standing on a platform of kindness, equality, addressing the climate emergency, investing in public services, and stopping a hard Brexit, change seemed in the air.

Growing up in Chingford

Faiza is the daughter of a Fijian car mechanic, with a Pakistani mother. She was born in the local, now crumbling, Whipps Cross hospital. Her mother called her Faiza because it means winner in Arabic.

Her mother met her father in Karachi, Pakistan, when he was on the run from the police. Not that she was aware of this, as he'd lied to her about what he was doing in the country. She was captivated by his 'incredible charm' and 'dark skin and light eyes'.[9] Her mother's family were against the match as they'd never heard of Fiji, and he'd already been married, with a son to another woman. But Faiza's mother was headstrong, in love and drawn to adventure. Her parents relented, agreeing to the marriage.

They planned to move to Canada, in search of a better life. At the last minute, Faiza's father changed the plan, insisting they go to the UK. Faiza's mother had no idea that the police had finally caught up with him. By the time they reached the UK, his picture was in the newspaper, wanted for kidnapping his son from his first marriage. By this time there was no turning back – Faiza's mother was already pregnant and thousands of miles away from home.

Faiza's father taught her to be proud of her heritage, and gave her long lectures on the crimes of the British Empire. When the Queen appeared on TV, he would explain how her crown jewels had been stolen from their ancestors and Africa. Even when caught sneaking sugar from the sugar bowl, rather than give her the usual parental speech about rotting teeth, he'd tell her about their family's history, picking sugar cane as indentured labour 100 years ago.

Despite this important political education, Faiza's father was a disaster for the family. 'He was dodgy. He was dodgy with money, dodgy with women, and dodgy with his fists,' Faiza explained.[10] Debt collectors and the police were regular visitors to their front door.

Faiza's childhood was one of fear. She feared her dad, feared her dad hitting her mum, feared her dad leaving and never coming back. She feared being kicked out of the house where she shared a single bed with her sister, huddled together against the cold under a tower of blankets; a house infested with damp and unfit for human habitation. The one thing she had was her academic ability. 'I knew from a young age this was my ticket out,' explained Faiza.[11]

When Faiza was only four years old, her mother was washing her in the bath and had something similar to a vision. In Urdu, she told her daughter: 'One day you'll go to Oxford. The best university in the world.'[12] Faiza attended the local state run primary school, and had never heard of this strange place. But an idea was planted in her head.

Facing racism

Growing up during the 80s and 90s, Fazia's father felt it was inevitable she'd face racism at school. Trying to channel the spirit of Muhammud Ali, he'd line Fazia and her sister up, telling them to take turns to hit him as hard as they could, in his belly or arm. 'When they call you Paki,' he said. 'You punch them like this.' He slammed his bare fist against the brick wall.[13] Meanwhile, her horrified mother offered a different approach. 'Just tell them, in Urdu, Paki means clean.' she suggested.[14] Her father laughed, and said her approach was useless.

It didn't take long before racist abuse was directed at Faiza in school. She was only five, but knew this was the moment she'd been preparing for all of her short life. So did she punch him like her father suggested, or talk her way out of it like her mother urged? In the end, she went with her mother's advice. Following his impromptu education in Urdu, the little boy was rendered speechless. When another child reported to a dinner lady that someone was being mean, Faiza was reminded that: 'Sticks and stones may break my bones but words will never hurt me.' This was the 80s approach to racism.

Although she didn't realise it at the time, that moment in the playground was life defining. Faiza learnt that she was going to have to stick up for herself, but she could do it in a way that suited her. A few decades later, this would play out on the national stage.

Mixing with the elite

When she was 18, Faiza fulfilled her mother's prophecy, securing a place at Oxford to study philosophy, politics and economics. Her mother said it was her destiny. While it was easy for Faiza to claim it was her mother's encouragement, and her own hard work, she knew community, supportive teachers, and financial help through welfare benefits all played their part. Then there was the luck at having a race expert in the room when she was interviewed.

The summer before she went to university, Faiza got a job in a mobile phone shop, which as a teenager got her a lot of street cred. It was in Camden, which gave her easy access to the vintage stores on the market. She took this bohemian wardrobe with her to Oxford, and on one of her first nights, dressed up in a colourful, ethnic inspired, outfit. She felt good as she strode out to the freshers' event. But it quickly became clear this was not the vibe of the evening. When someone asked her what school she went to, she replied with the name of her local East London college. This wasn't the correct answer. As she observed others, she realised the room was being divided into those who went to Eton, Harrow, Westminster, Winchester or Charterhouse; and those who didn't.

Despite feeling out of place, Faiza graduated with flying colours. She went on to do a Masters and PhD at Manchester University, which launched a high-profile career in policy and research. Her work continued to put her in rooms with the elite, where the only people who looked like her were serving the food. Sometimes they seemed to forget she was there entirely, spewing out racist and offensive comments, or talking openly about the backhand, corrupt deals their extreme privileged brought them.

While this triumph over adversity story can feel like something from the movies, Faiza is keen to point out: 'My story is not a nice story. It is one of desperation.'[15] She is also painfully aware that many of the resources that were there to support her, have since been decimated by the Conservative government. While it's seductive to believe these rags to riches stories can happen to anyone, Faiza believes that focusing only on the exceptions at the top, means we end up ignoring the declining conditions at the bottom. The barriers to success for working class women like her are only getting higher, and the hard work required is increasingly unrealistic. It also reinforces a hierarchy of importance, where we diminish the value of our cleaners, supermarket workers, carers and other people the 2020 lockdown proved are invaluable to keep society going.

This was personal

While Faiza's career was booming, her personal life was heading toward a crisis. Faiza's mother struggled with a deteriorating heart condition for 10 years. There were multiple visits to hospital, and she reached a point where she could no longer walk across a room without struggling for breath. On top of that, her mother was one of the thousands of sick and disabled people who'd been on the receiving end of benefit cuts. She'd had assessors knocking on her door, putting her through a series of demeaning questions about her health. 'It made her feel like a criminal,' Faiza said. 'It still makes my heart hurt when I think about the stress and humiliation she endured.'[16]

In 2016, they heard she'd finally made it on to the transplant list, and was scheduled for surgery. 'At last, after everything she had gone through with my Dad and her health, this was her chance at happiness,' Faiza said.[17]

Three months later they were back in A&E. A few weeks after, she died. When cleaning out her mother's house after her death, Faiza found folders full of correspondence to the benefits office, pleading her case. She'd also begged the local council for more social care support. 'I cried for hours packing up the house,' Faiza said. 'Not just because I missed her, but because she had suffered more than she needed to as a result of ill-conceived policies designed by people who had little empathy for those struggling.'[18] As far as Faiza was concerned, Iain Duncan Smith's policies had made her mother's final years a misery, adding stress that had likely contributed to her early death.

When Faiza decided to stand for election, it wasn't just to provide voters with a socialist alternative to Tory rule. She was fighting for justice for her mother, and all the other families who'd found themselves destroyed by austerity.

2019 election

At 1am on election night, Faiza's campaigner manager told her to get to the Waltham Forest town hall. Things were looking good, he told her. This surprised Faiza, as the exit polls for Labour had been abysmal. If they were correct, the Tories were on course for a massive majority.

When she arrived at the town hall, she could feel the tension. Stacks of ballot papers piled high on desks, with weary looking officials packing up after five hours of counting. A few smiled at her, betraying their political allegiances. Faiza held her breath as the returning officer mounted the stage to declare the result.

The people had spoken. Faiza had done well – 22,219 votes – a 17 point increase on her vote share, compared to the 2015 Labour Party candidate. But it wasn't enough. Iain Duncan Smith scrapped in with a majority of just 1,262 votes.

'There is no justice,' Faiza repeated over and over in her head, as she watched her rival head to the podium to give his victory speech.[19]

In the aftermath of her defeat, Faiza battled with her inner critic, emboldened by outer social pressures. Who did she think she was, this working class, Muslim woman trying to take on a wealthy man who lived in a mansion and was married to a baron's daughter? Statistics were her business, and she knew the odds on someone from her background becoming an MP were slim. Yet she also knew elections are shaped by various factors, so in 2024 she stood again.

The betrayal

Faiza spent the next five years out on the streets, knocking on doors nearly every week. She was determined not to be one of the politicians that people only saw around election time, but instead actively listening to constituent's problems. She campaigned to save South Chingford library, where she'd spent so much time as a child, reading the books they couldn't afford to have at home, and escaping the chaos of family life; she promised voters she'd protect the high street where she'd had her first job at the local Greggs; address local infrastructure problems that held up in traffic the same buses she took; she fought for families facing eviction; and visited local colleges to support young people who were in the same place she had once been.

When Prime Minister, Rishi Sunak, finally called the election on 22nd May 2024, Faiza was ready. Her reputation in the area was strong, and although local polling is known to be unreliable, results suggested she had a good chance to finally take the seat.

A week later, the shocking news came that the Labour Party had deselected her as a parliamentary candidate. Appearing on BBC's Newsnight the following evening, she appeared visibly shaken, and close to tears. 'I'm so shocked right now, to be treated so badly, after being such an active member of the party,' she told the broadcaster.[20]

Channel 4 News later obtained exclusive audio recording of Faiza's interview with Labour's National Executive Committee (NEC), held before she was formally deselected. She was allegedly given only a few hours to prepare, leaving her unable to find childcare for her small baby. In the recording, she is clearly struggling to manage her infant, who is crying loudly. You can hear her saying: 'My baby can feel my stress.'[21]

On the call, three NEC members presented social media activity dating back a decade. They accused her of liking some posts that downplayed anti semitism. One of the tweets was a sketch from the Daily Show about Israel. On hearing the news, Jon Stewart tweeted: 'This is the dumbest thing the UK has done since electing Boris Johnson ... 'Another of Faiza's tweets featured a photo of her standing with Jeremy Corbyn, which was twisted to suggest she was proud of the antisemitism in that era. She was also criticised for social media content relating to her experiences of Islamophobia in the party. The Labour Muslim Network said using this as evidence to deselect her was 'utterly outrageous.'[22]

Faiza's deselection followed a number of other socialist candidates being told they couldn't stand, and veteran MP, Diane Abbott, being on indefinite suspension. Following accusations that Labour was purging left wing candidates, party leader, Kier Stamer denied the allegations saying he only wanted the 'highest quality candidates'.[23] Yet Faiza was one of the few to increase Labour's vote share in 2019, and looked on track to land a historic victory in her constituency.

A week later, she wrote an article in The Guardian saying that four years work had been thrown in the bin, and her connection to the community brushed aside. She revealed months of bullying by the party, including being stripped of a paid organiser when seven months pregnant. 'I should have known this was coming,' she said.[24]

The BBC reported that 50 Chingford and Woodford Green Labour Party members cancelled their membership, citing Faiza's treatment as their reason. Seven Labour councillors also resigned. In an open letter they expressed their 'disillusionment and anger' at the Labour leadership, and the party's 'institutional racism.'[25]

Following her Newsnight interview, hundreds of people got in touch to express their support, saying they would no longer vote Labour. The public was angry, as they knew the chances of booting out Iain Duncan Smith had now diminished. While Labour parachuted another candidate in, she had no connection to the community and was virtually unknown. But Faiza was not ready to give up. Just as she'd found her own way of dealing with racist bullies when she was five years old, Faiza dealt with Labour in her own way. She announced she'd resigned from the party and was standing as an independent candidate.

In a statement Faiza said: 'I have reached a decision following hundreds of messages from people in my community, who say there are no options left for them. They are tired of the Tories but now feel they can't trust Labour.'[26]

The campaign continued, but sadly it wouldn't be enough. The Labour Party had split the vote. Their candidate, Shama Tatler, and Faiza received around 12,000 votes each, letting Iain Duncan Smith squeeze in between with 17,281. On election night, Faiza smiled stiffly as her result was announced, the emotion barely held back. When Tatler's result came in, Faiza turned to her and shook her head.[27] In a statement she said: 'They [the Labour Party] let my community down. I'm so angry with them right now. That shouldn't have happened.'[28]

Today, Faiza continues to fight for the people of Chingford and Woodford Green. 'This is my home, the community that made me and I'm not going anywhere.' She has pledged to keep campaigning, gathering ideas, and holding the Labour Party to account.[29]

Faiza's legacy

Considering Faiza's caution around rags to riches stories, calling her an inspirational figure for other women from minority backgrounds, may not be appropriate. Yet in her book, Know Your Place, she says that knowledge is power. She wants to empower others to argue against the current narrative around social mobility, offering an alternative that values everybody. The book ends with a smart and manageable list of action points that could do just that.

These are arguments many do not want made public. Attempts to silence her have been massive, but with her irrepressible spirit and intelligence it's unlikely she will be held down long. It's hard not to see her David and Goliath story in cinematic terms – there are so many dramatic twists and betrayals – but it feels like an unfinished story. Let's hope for the people of Chingford & Woodford Green, Faiza continues to rise up.

Conclusion

On 25th November 2024, a petition on the government's website launched, demanding Sir Kier Starmer call another election. Within days it reached nearly three million signatures. When asked about it on ITV's This Morning, Starmer pointed out that this is not how democracy works – you don't get a 'best of three'.

Yet within the first few months of Labour's new term, the public tension and frustration was palpable. Adult children urged their elderly parents to get the right forms completed to ensure they didn't lose their winter fuel allowance; disabled people took to social media voicing their fears around losing life saving benefits; and food bank workers pointed to their growing queues and overworked staff. The British public simply can't be expected to wait another four years until they are allowed to speak again. Something has to be done. The issue is, what?

One of the most damaging impacts of neo-liberalism and the decline of the trade union movement, is that people have lost their sense of agency and the ability to change anything. Cries of 'all politicians are the same' and 'nothing ever changes' are frequently heard, from mumbles in the corners of pubs, to shrieks on social media.

To make matters worse, the solidarity movements of the past have been replaced by woke culture. This places social values ahead of economic and political factors, with a strict and often complex moral code. If an individual falls foul of this code, they are socially shamed, or even labelled as racist, sexist or transphobic. While the woke movement started from legitimate grievances, it's spiralled into an obsession with language and weaponised victimhood.

I once fell foul of this moral code myself, and was publicly shamed for it. A fellow activist had posted something on Facebook. I thought it was an interesting post that reflected some things I'd been thinking. I left a comment saying so. But I was a white woman commenting on a brown woman's issues. Something in my turn of phrase offended her. Instead of calmly pointing it out so I could understand, she published a blog about me. While I wasn't named, it was clearly me she referred to. She posted it on her Facebook page, with that favourite passive aggressive phrase: 'I'll just leave this here'. I can only assume she hoped I would see it, which of course I did. I was hurt, and embarrassed, and needless to say, we never campaigned together again.

There are much bigger issues to the fall out of woke culture than my pride. While I was able to find other spaces to organise in, many others will turn to extremists. In an interview on Pod Save The UK, YouTuber, JimmytheGiant, explained how he got sucked into alt-right content on the video sharing site. 'They said "conservativism is the new punk". You were the different guy. If you were right-wing, and in a group of people your age, and they start talking about Jeremy Corbyn, you might say, "actually, nationalisation is inefficient …"'

JimmytheGiant followed people like Joe Rogan, Joe Shapiro and even Tommy Robinson, sucked in by their rhetoric. He explained: 'I've always liked new ideas. When I was younger I put trust into that. That must mean it is correct.' It was when they started talking about Ukraine, which he has a personal connection to (his wife is Ukrainian) that he started to query what they were telling him. His curious mind asked questions, and he was able to pull himself out of what he calls 'the pipeline'. Not everyone will have that. Various studies show that Generation Z men in particular are lurching towards the right.[1] Some have put Reform UK's success in the 2024 election down to the 'bro vote' due to Farage's popularity on Tik Tok.[2]

Woke culture also risks slowing down progress. For commercial corporations, appearing woke is an easy win. They can agree to a change in language, and putting up some rainbow flags during Pride month. Or in the case of British Airways, sponsoring the Pride march. This is easier than changing their business model, supporting workers to unionise, or taking responsibility for the impact of their corporate behaviour.

While well meaning, woke culture is ultimately damaging our ability to create social change. It's forcing us into smaller and smaller groups, as victims compete against each other in a hierarchy of oppression. If you come from a minority position, you are far better to find commonality with others, than argue about who has it worse. As Ash Sarkar says in Minority Rule, we don't have to ignore the brutality of racism, sexism, ableism, homophobia and transphobia. 'But if we continue to insist that minorities can fight alone, we are consigning ourselves to losing alone.'[3]

This is why looking to our past is so important. The stories within this book give solid examples of how people working together, sometimes across different issues, creates meaningful change. The East London suffragettes understood this. They didn't differentiate between pay equality, housing issues, sexual harassment, and the right to vote. It was all interconnected to them. Milly Witkops and Rudolph Rocker drew lines between garment workers and dockers, bringing thousands out on strike in a mass act of solidarity. Lesbian & Gays Support the Miners didn't disappear into their own silos. They made an unlikely alliance by drawing on, and clearly articulating, the parallels between their oppression and that of the miners. Later, the Battle of Claremont Road drew together everyone from homeless people, to middle class suburbanites, with ravers, hunt saboteurs and environmentalists in between. Looking to the fights we're facing today, those keen to only identify as trans rights activists, or disability campaigners, fail to see they are only two short steps away from each other. Both need bodily autonomy and more investment in the NHS.

But when we look to the past to learn lessons, we have to ask, whose voices do we listen to? While researching this book, I interviewed a number of women politicians. A strong theme ran through their stories: they believed that unless you are in the seat of power, you can't make change. While obviously they are the only ones in positions to formulate legislation, it's too simplistic to say that parliament is the only route to changing society. Furthermore, meaningful change often comes from the bottom up; from the people whose lives these policies so irrevocably impact. We see this through the stories of Muriel and Doris Lester, and the other women who created the foundations for the welfare state through their home-help schemes. When these communities are excluded, any steps forward in women's equality leaves too many others behind. This was evident in the votes for women campaign, where the middle class more or less abandoned working-class communities, leaving them without the vote for a further decade. We saw it again with the Carnival Against Capitalist, whose joyous approach to societal change became a movement only for those physically, socially, emotionally and financially able to join.

Yet finding the voices of these women from the grassroots was one of the biggest challenges I had with my research. Some, like Faiza Shaheen, had the opportunity to publish a book, and the courage to share her personal story. Most working-class women will not. Resources like letters and diaries are usually inaccessible too, as most archives will not keep them unless the person is deemed notable enough (as a side note, this is also the criteria for English Heritage blue plaques, which could do with a review too). I'm enormously thankful for the hard work and generous spirit of the Bishopsgate Institute, who take a different approach. They see the value and importance of ordinary people's personal effects in helping us understand their thoughts and beliefs, so that we might better understand our own lives. The endless hours I spent in their (extremely cold!) reading room is a big reason the lives of the women in this book are so fully realised.

Women have been too long excluded from our historical narratives, especially those from working class backgrounds. Yet we need these stories. Although this book contains a fraction of the voices we should hear, we can still learn a lot from them. There are many more fights ahead of us. There are new rights to win, and rights we thought we had won will come under threat again. By learning about our past we gain ideas, inspiration and strategies to help us fight back and find a path to victory.

THE END

Notes

Introduction

1. Oral history interview at part of the Women Activists of East London project archived at The Bishopsgate Institute
2. David Rosenberg, *Rebel Footprints: a guide to uncovering London's Radical History* (2015)

Chapter 1: Match Women Rise Up!

1. Samuel Webster oral history, archived at the British Library.
2. We do not have accurate records of the ages of all those who went on strike, but it was fairly common for working class children to be out at work by the age of 12.
3. https://en.wikipedia.org/wiki/Bryant_%26_May, accessed 16th June 2022
4. Louise Raw, *Striking A Light* (2011), p92–102
5. Oral histories taken from Louise Raw, *Striking A Light* (2011)
6. J. Charlton, British Weekly Commissioners *Toilers in London (*1889)
7. A. Wood Besant *Annie Besant* (1893)
8. Anon, probably M Harkness *(1889)* cited in J Charlton, British Weekly Commissioners, *Toilers in London (1889)* p21
9. Following a merger with the Amalgamated Society of Boilermakers, Shipwrights, Blacksmiths and Structural Workers (ASBSBSW), the union was renamed the General, Municipal, Boilermakers and Allied Trade Union GMBATU). This was shortened to GMB, which in 1987 became its official name.
10. https://www.matchgirls1888.org/saving-sarah-chapmans-grave accessed 23rd June 2022
11. The Commonweal 21st July 1888
12. Paul Thompson *Socialist Liberals and Labour: The Struggle for London 1855–1914 (1967)*, p45
13. T Mann *Memoirs* (1923) p203
14. Louise Raw, *Striking A Light* (2011) p158
15. Ibid, p77
16. https://www.matchgirls1888.org/matchgirls-statue accessed 23rd June 2022
17. At time of writing other plans were afoot by the Matchgirls Memorial Campaign, including musicals, children's books and an annual commemoration in the House of Lords.

Chapter 2: Milly Rise Up!

1. https://pasttenseblog.wordpress.com/2017/02/03/today-in-londons-radical-history-jewish-anarchist-club-opens-in-jubilee-street-whitechapel-1906/ accessed 29th June 2022
2. I have been unable to verify what a patch cutter is, despite extensive research. One theory is that this was a typo, and should have read pattern cutter. Tailoring was a common trade within the Jewish community.

3. http://www.dadaweb.de/wiki/Witkop,_Milly accessed 29th June 2022

4. https://www.bl.uk/victorian-britain/articles/the-working-classes-and-the-poor, accessed 25th Jan 2023

5. Rudolph Rocker, *Milly Witkop-Rocker* (1956))

6. https://lbhflibraries.wordpress.com/2016/10/27/rose-witcop/, accessed 30th June 2022

7. Rudolph Rocker, *Milly Witkop-Rocker* (1956)

8. https://libcom.org/article/1912-year-strikes-east-end-london, accessed 6th July 2022

9. http://solfed.org.uk/da/the-workers-friend-rudolf-rocker-and-the-arbeter-fraint-jewish-anarchist-group-in-the-east-end-of, accessed 6th July 2022

10. Janine Booth, *Minnie Lansbury: Suffragette, Socialist and Rebel councillor* (2018), p107

11. East London Advertiser, 14th October 1916

12. Rudolph Rocker, *Milly Witkop-Rocker* (1956)

13. https://eastendwomensmuseum.org/blog/milly-witkop, accessed 30th June 2022

14. Rudolph Rocker, *Milly Witkop-Rocker* (1956)

15. Ibid

16. Eleanor Marx was Karl Marx's daughter; May Morris was William Morris' daughter; and Margaret McDonald was the wife of British Labour Party Leader and Prime Minister, Ramsay McDonald. All were politically active, with great achievements of their own. They rarely get the same prominence as the men in their lives.

Chapter 3: Adelaide Rise Up!

1. Winifred Langton and Fay Jacobsen, *Courage: An account of the lives of Eliza Adellaide Knight and Donald Adophus Brown* (2007), p16

2. Ibid, p66

3. Ibid, p78

4. Ibid, p110

5. Ibid, p110

6. Ibid, p112

7. Ibid, p114

8. Katherine Connnelly, *Sylvia Pankhurst: Suffragette, socialist and scourge of the empire*, Pluto Press (2013), p58–59

9. Winifred Langton and Fay Jacobsen, *Courage: An account of the lives of Eliza Adelaide Knight and Donald Adophus Brown* (2007), p120

10. Ibid p120

11. Sarah Jackson and Rosemary Taylor, *East London Suffragettes*, The History Press (2014), p77

12. David Rosenberg, *Rebel Footprints: a guide to uncovering London's Radical History* (2015)

13. Katherine Connnelly, *Sylvia Pankhurst: Suffragette, socialist and scourge of the empire*, Pluto Press (2013), p66

Chapter 4: Eva Rise Up!

1. Extracts mostly taken from *Dear Girl: The diaries and letters of two working women 1897–1917*, edited by Tierl Thompson (1987) and some directly from Eva's diaries.

2. Tierl Thompson, *Dear Girl: The diaries and letters of two working women 1897–1917* (1987), p118

3. Ibid, p172

4. Ibid, p177–8

5. Emma Donoghue, *Termagant from Furies: Stories of the wild, wicked and untamed* (2023) p72
6. Tierl Thompson, Dear Girl: The diaries and letters of two working women 1897–1917 (1987), p151
7. Ibid, p174
8. Ibid, p163
9. Ibid, p154
10. Ibid, p161
11. Eva Slawson diary, 18/2/14
12. Eva Slawson diary, 19/2/14
13. Tierl Thompson, Dear Girl: The diaries and letters of two working women 1897–1917 (1987), p281
14. Ibid, p294
15. Ibid, p299
16. Minna Simmons letter to Ruth Slate, 28/1/17
17. Minna Simmons letter to Ruth Slate, 26/2/17
18. Rebecca Jennings, *A Lesbian History of Britain: love and sex between women since 1500*, Greenwood World publishing (2007)
19. Martha Vicinus *"They wonder to which sex I belong" The Historical Roots of the Modern Lesbian Identity*, Lesbian & Gay Studies Reader (1993)
20. https://evanstheblogs.blogspot.com/2018/09/mm-mf-go-camping.html, accessed 21st May 2024

Chapter 5: Minnie Rise Up!
1. Charles Booth poverty map and notebooks (1898), p127
2. Janine Booth, *Minnie Lansbury: Suffragette, Socialist and Rebel Councillor* (2018), p24
3. Ibid, p35–42
4. Jenny Keating, *History in Education* (2010)
5. Janine Booth, Minnie *Lansbury: Suffragette, Socialist and Rebel Councillo*r (2018), p49
6. Ibid, p55
7. Ibid, p68
8. East End News, 31st May 1935
9. https://en.wikipedia.org/wiki/George_Lansbury, accessed 27th June 2024
10. Janine Booth, *Minnie Lansbury: Suffragette, Socialist and Rebel Councillo*r (2018), p74
11. Martin Gottfried, *Balancing Act: The Authorised Biography of Angela Lansbury* (1999), p4
12. Pankhurst 1932 p132–3
13. The Women's Dreadnought, 17th April and 11th September 1915
14. Edgar Lansbury's appeal, 13th September 1917
15. Bessie Lansbury letter, 29th January 1918
16. Janine Booth, *Minnie Lansbury: Suffragette, Socialist and Rebel Councillo*r (2018), p114
17. Aberdeen Journal, 25th August 1921
18. The Times, 6th September 1921
19. Janine Booth, *Minnie Lansbury: Suffragette, Socialist and Rebel Councillo*r (2018), p206

Chapter 6: Muriel Rise Up!
1. Muriel Lester, *It Occurred to Me* (1937), p5
2. Ibid, p2

3. Ibid, p19

4. Ibid, p13

5. Ibid, p7

6. Ibid, p35

7. Ibid, 145

8. https://eastlondonwomen.org.uk/, accessed 3rd January 2024

9. Share UK, *Beyond Medicine: A social History of Women and Pandemics* (2023), p7

10. Muriel Lester, *It Occurred to Me* (1937), p44

11. Ibid, p45–45

12. Ibid, p52

13. Ibid, p53

14. http://muriellester.org/kh_origins.html, accessed 28th September 2024

15. Muriel Lester, *It Occurred to Me* (1937), p63

16. Ibid, p65

17. Ibid, p78–79

18. Ibid, p78

19. Ibid, p100

20. Oral history interview with Sylvia Bishop, Kingsley Hall archives

21. Muriel Lester, *It Occurred to Me* (1937), p108

22. https://news-archive.hud.ac.uk/news/allstories/globalaudiencefordiamondjubileeprofe ssor.php, accessed 24th September 2024

23. Muriel Lester, *It Occurred to Me* (1937), p129

24. Ibid, p135

25. Ibid, p167

26. Ibid, p170

27. https://www.thetimes.com/article/gandhi-an-inspiration-or-a-sexual-predator-k8jrkqw7vc3, accessed 3rd October 2024

28. Muriel Lester, It So Happened (1947), p18

29. https://www.iwm.org.uk/history/london-in-the-second-world-war, accessed 29th July 2024

30. *Bethnal Green: Building and Social Conditions from 1915 to 1945, A History of the County of Middlesex* Volume 11: Stepney, Bethnal Green (1998) p132–135

31. Rosemary Taylor and Christopher Lloyd, *The East End at War,* Sutton Publishing (2007)

32. Muriel Lester, *It So Happened* (1947), p135

33. Ibid, p137

34. Ibid, p163

35. Ibid, p195

36. Ibid, p204

37. https://www.bishopsgate.org.uk/collections/lester-muriel-christian-pacifist, accessed 17th October 2024

38. https://en.wikipedia.org/wiki/Muriel_Lester#:~:text=She%20was%20recognized%20 as%20one,not%20kept%20prior%20to%201939.), accessed 17th October 2024

39. http://news.bbc.co.uk/local/london/hi/people_and_places/history/newsid_ 8077000/8077217.stm, accessed 17the October 2024

40. Oral history with Sylvia Bishopp, http://muriellester.org/ohssb.html, accessed 17th October 2024

41. https://www.theguardian.com/books/2012/sep/02/rd-laing-mental-health-sanity, accessed 17th October 2024

42. https://en.wikipedia.org/wiki/Kingsley_Hall, accessed 17th October 2024

Chapter 7: Hetty Rise Up!

1. Canonbury was moved from the borough of Hackney to Islington in a boundary change in 1993

2. https://www.british-history.ac.uk/vch/middx/vol10/pp145-148#anchorn18, accessed 23rd July 2024

3. Charles Booth notebooks, BOOTH/B/347, p27

4. Annie Barnes, *Tough Annie: from suffragette to Stepney councillor* (1980) p14

5. David Rosenberg, *Battle for the East End* (2011), p22

6. https://www.stopwar.org.uk/article/what-kept-hetty-bower-campaigning-for-peace-and-justice-for-over-ninety-years/, accessed 29th July 2024

7. David Rosenberg, *Battle for the East End* (2011), p25

8. https://www.theguardian.com/commentisfree/2012/jun/29/conversation-life-after-age-100, accessed 29the July 2024

9. https://www.bbc.co.uk/programmes/p00r3qkt, accessed 24th July 2024

10. Ibid

11. David Rosenberg, Battle for the East End (2011), p37

12. Ibid, p38

13. Ibid, p141

14. Hansard 5.3.36

15. David Rosenberg, *Battle for the East End* (2011), p201

16. Ibid, p197

17. Daily Mirror, Monday 5th October 1936

18. Oral history interview with Beattie Orwell, recorded 24th April 2016, archived at The Bishopsgate Institute as part of the Women Activists of East London collection.

19. https://irr.org.uk/article/new-writing-on-cable-street/ accessed 23rd July 2024

20. https://www.mirror.co.uk/news/uk-news/hetty-bower-dies-aged-108-2789490, accessed 3rd February 2024

21. Interview with Charlie Goodman, archived at The Imperial War Museum

22. https://eastendwomensmuseum.org/blog/women-at-the-battle-of-cable-street, accessed 24th July 2024

23. Searchlight, October 1996

24. Daily Herald, Monday 5th October 1936

25. Ibid

26. Oral history interview with Beattie Orwell, recorded 24th April 2016, archived at The Bishopsgate Institute as part of the Women Activists of East London collection.

27. David Rosenberg, *Battle for the East End* (2011), p239

28. Daily Mirror, 5th October 1936

29. https://www.stopwar.org.uk/article/what-kept-hetty-bower-campaigning-for-peace-and-justice-for-over-ninety-years/, accessed 29th July 2024

30. Life in Hackney London, WW2 People's War, 2nd December 2005

31. https://www.yadvashem.org/righteous/stories/czech-republic.html, accessed 29th July 2024

32. https://www.independent.co.uk/news/obituaries/hetty-bower-political-activist-whose-membership-of-the-labour-party-stretched-back-to-the-days-of-keir-hardie-8943292.html, accessed 29the July 2024

33. https://cnduk.org/peoples-history-of-cnd-easter-marches-to-aldermaston-1958-60/, accessed 3rd February 2025

34. https://www.mirror.co.uk/news/uk-news/hetty-bower-dies-aged-108-2789490, accessed 29th July 2024

35. https://www.theguardian.com/world/2004/oct/07/usa.iraq1, accessed 14th November 2024

36. https://www.theguardian.com/world/2003/sep/07/usa.theobserver, accessed 29th July 2024

37. https://web.archive.org/web/20090126150127/http://www.gallup-international.com/ContentFiles/survey.asp?id=10, accessed 29th July 2024

38. https://www.stopwar.org.uk/about/, accessed 14/11/24

39. The police estimated 750,000 people marched, but the BBC estimated it was more like a million. Either way, it was far larger than the 500,000 originally predicted.

40. https://en.wikipedia.org/wiki/15_February_2003_anti-war_protests#cite_ref-6, accessed 29th July 2024.

41. https://thequietus.com/culture/books/seumas-milne-revenge-history-interview/, accessed 29th July 2024

42. Women Activists of East London ran between 2015 and 2020 and is archived at the Bishopsgate Institute.

43. https://www.stopwar.org.uk/article/what-kept-hetty-bower-campaigning-for-peace-and-justice-for-over-ninety-years/, accessed 29th July 2024

44. https://www.mirror.co.uk/news/uk-news/hetty-bower-dies-aged-108-2789490, accessed 29th July 2024

45. https://oursouthend.wordpress.com/2013/11/13/a-remarkable-woman-and-campaigner-hetty-bower-1905-2013/, accessed 29th July 2024

46. https://www.theguardian.com/world/2013/nov/29/hetty-bower, accessed 29th July 2024

47. https://www.camdennewjournal.co.uk/article/the-world-is-diminished-by-the-loss-of-hetty-bower-and-margie-dolan, accessed 29th July 2024

Chapter 8: Ellen Rise Up!

1. Oral history interview, part of the Women Activists of East London project archived at the Bishopsgate Institute

2. https://www.theguardian.com/uk/2006/sep/05/greenham5, accessed 30th July 2024

3. https://commonwealarchives.wordpress.com/2010/08/31/peace-camping/, accessed 30th July 2024

4. https://www.iwm.org.uk/partnerships/subject-specialist-network/connecting-sharing-learning-project/we-say-no-to-the-bomb, accessed 30th July 2024

5. https://www.theguardian.com/uk/2006/sep/05/greenham5, accessed 30th July 2024

6. https://en.wikipedia.org/wiki/Greenham_Common_Women%27s_Peace_Camp#CITEREFShepherd2010, accessed 30th July 2024

7. Original words by Naomi Little Bear, additional lyrics by the women of Greenham

8. https://en.wikipedia.org/wiki/Greenham_Common_Women%27s_Peace_Camp#CITEREFShepherd2010, accessed 30th July 2024

9. https://www.theguardian.com/uk/2006/sep/05/greenham5, accessed 30th July 2024.

10. http://news.bbc.co.uk/onthisday/hi/dates/stories/april/1/newsid_2520000/2520753.stm, accessed 30th July 2024

11. http://www.greenhamwpc.org.uk/historic.htm, accessed 30th July 2024

12. https://womenslibrary.org.uk/2021/08/18/the-greenham-common-womens-peace-camp/, accessed 30th July 2024

Chapter 9: Anny Rise Up!
1. Spare Rib, No.89, July 1979
2. https://en.wikipedia.org/wiki/Stonewall_riots, accessed 31st July 2024
3. Ibid
4. Ibid
5. Ibid
6. Ibid
7. Spare Rib No. 89, July 1979
8. Jeffrey Weeks, Coming Out: The Emergence of LGBT identities in Britain from the nineteenth century to the present (2016), p187
9. https://academic.oup.com/hwj/article/83/1/79/3862507, accessed 31st July 2024
10. Ibid, p89
11. Ibid, p91
12. Ibid, p89
13. Spare Rib No. 89 July 1979
14. Come Together, no 10, p6
15. Spare Rib No. 89 July 1979
16. Ibid
17. https://eige.europa.eu/publications-resources/toolkits-guides/gender-equality-index-2021-report/gender-differences-household-chores , accessed 31st July 2023

Chapter 10: Jane Rise Up!
1. Oral history interview, part of the Women Activists of East London project archived at the Bishopsgate Institute
2. https://liberatinghistories.org/periodicals-guide/shocking-pink/, accessed 1st August 2024
3. http://lgsm.org/about-lgsm, accessed 1st August 2024
4. https://www.rs21.org.uk/2014/09/21/dear-love-of-comrades-remembering-lesbians-and-gays-support-the-miners/, accessed 1st August 2024
5. https://blogs.lse.ac.uk/lsehistory/2024/02/28/women-against-pit-closures-the-jean-mccrindle-archives/, accessed 1st August 2024
6. https://www.rs21.org.uk/2014/09/21/dear-love-of-comrades-remembering-lesbians-and-gays-support-the-miners/, accessed 1st August 2024
7. https://en.wikipedia.org/wiki/1984%E2%80%931985_United_Kingdom_miners%27_strike#cite_ref-8, accessed 1st August 2024
8. https://fullfact.org/economy/wage-growth-napoleonic-wars/, accessed 1st August 2024
9. All Out! Dancing in the Dulais
10. https://economicsociology.org/2018/03/19/thatcherisms-greatest-achievement/, accessed 1st August 2024
11. https://www.bbc.co.uk/news/business-19521535, accessed 1st August 2024
12. https://www.tuc.org.uk/news/tuc-welcomes-90000-rise-trade-union-membership, accessed 1st August 2024

Chapter 11: Olive Rise Up!
1. Oral history interview with Mike McColgan archived at https://olivemorris.org/, accessed 2nd August 2024
2. https://en.wikipedia.org/wiki/Olive_Morris#cite_note-DHC-13, accessed 2nd August 2024

3. https://rememberolivemorris.wordpress.com/category/black-panthers/, accessed 2nd August 2024

4. https://en.wikipedia.org/wiki/Olive_Morris#cite_note-DHC-13, accessed 2nd August 2024

5. https://www.bristol.ac.uk/history/public-engagement/blackhistory/snapshots2021/eomorris/, accessed 2nd August 2024

6. https://mixedmuseum.org.uk/btcotc/the-grunwick-strike/, accessed 2nd August 2024

7. The Morning Star, 29th October 2009

8. https://libcom.org/article/radical-history-121-railton-road-lambeth, accessed 2nd August 2024

9. Oral history interview with Mike McColgan 'Remembering Olive Morris' IV/279. Held at Lambeth Archives.

10. Ibid

11. https://uomhistory.com/2019/10/13/black-women-who-have-struggled-to-make-our-efforts-possible-olive-morris-and-the-legacy-of-black-power-in-manchester/#_ftnref14, accessed 2nd August 2024

12. https://en.wikipedia.org/wiki/Olive_Morris#cite_note-DHC-13, accessed 2nd August 2024

13. https://rememberolivemorris.wordpress.com/category/activism/, accessed 2nd August 2024

14. https://en.wikipedia.org/wiki/Olive_Morris#cite_note-DHC-13, accessed 2nd August 2024

15. Oral history interview with Mike McColgan archived at https://olivemorris.org/, accessed 2nd August 2024

16. https://journals.sagepub.com/doi/10.1177/01417789211041898, accessed 2nd August 2024

17. Ibid

18. https://en.wikipedia.org/wiki/Olive_Morris#cite_note-DHC-13, accessed 2nd August 2024

19. https://rememberolivemorris.wordpress.com/wp-content/uploads/2021/04/dyrom_obi_.pdf, accessed 2nd August 2024

20. https://olivemorris.org/Awards, accessed 2nd August 2024

Chapter 12: Julie Rise Up!

1. Oral history interview at part of the Women Activists of East London project archived at The Bishopsgate Institute

2. Robert Winder, *Bloody Foreigners: The story of immigration to Britain* (2005), p196

3. 'Just a part of the wall', Homeless Bengali Women in Tower Hamlets, 8

4. https://spitalfieldslife.com/2024/02/18/julie-begum-someone-still-evolving-i/, accessed 13th August 2024

5. https://whitechapellondon.co.uk/bengali-squatters-movement-brick-lane/, accessed 13th August 2024

6. https://eastendwomensmuseum.org/blog/mala-sen-writer-and-race-equality-activist, accessed 13th August 2024

7. https://whitechapellondon.co.uk/bengali-squatters-movement-brick-lane/, accessed 13th August 2024

8. Spare Rib, December 1983, No. 137 p10

9. John Marriott, *Beyond the Tower: A History of East London* (2011)
10. https://eastendwomensmuseum.org/blog/mala-sen-writer-and-race-equality-activist, accessed 13th August 2024
11. https://www.thawra.co.uk/opinion/julie-begum-activism-bengali-community, accessed 13th August 2024
12. https://www.altabalifoundation.org.uk/articles/How_Altab_Ali_Changed_Us(JB).pdf accessed 13th August 2024
13. https://spitalfieldslife.com/2024/02/18/julie-begum-someone-still-evolving-i/, accessed 13th August 2024
14. https://en.wikipedia.org/wiki/Derek_Beackon, accessed 13th August 2024
15. https://nijjormanush.com/save-brick-lane-campaign/, accessed 13th August 2024

Chapter 13: Sonali Rise Up!

1. Oral history interview at part of the Women Activists of East London project archived at The Bishopsgate Institute
2. https://www.theguardian.com/uk/2000/jan/30/race.world2, accessed 7/11/24
3. Ibid
4. Ibid
5. Ibid
6. Oral history interview at part of the Women Activists of East London project archived at The Bishopsgate Institute
7. Ibid
8. Ibid
9. Rebel Women, Greenham Common Women's Peace Camp Pt 2, 3rd November 2021 (Share UK)
10. Oral history interview at part of the Women Activists of East London project archived at The Bishopsgate Institute
11. https://www.theguardian.com/uk/2000/jan/30/race.world2, accessed 7th November 2024
12. https://www.independent.co.uk/news/uk/crime/i-was-threatened-with-hanging-by-racist-prison-guards-180856.html, accessed 7th November 2024
13. Ibid
14. Oral history interview at part of the Women Activists of East London project archived at The Bishopsgate Institute
15. Ibid
16. Ibid
17. Ibid
18. https://blogs.lse.ac.uk/politicsandpolicy/british-public-opinion-after-a-decade-of-war-attitudes-to-iraq-and-afghanistan/, accessed 14th November 2024
19. https://www.theguardian.com/uk-news/2016/jul/06/iraq-inquiry-key-points-from-the-chilcot-report, accessed 14the November 2024
20. https://www.theguardian.com/uk-news/2016/jul/06/david-cameron-uk-must-never-repeat-iraq-war-mistakes, accessed 14th November 2024
21. https://www.amnesty.org.uk/blogs/campaigns-blog/political-awakening-new-play-prevent, accessed 26th March 2025
22. Oral history interview at part of the Women Activists of East London project archived at The Bishopsgate Institute

Chapter 14: Ziggy Rise Up!
1. Throughline, The Mandela Effect (podcast), 16th May 2024 (NPR)
2. Ibid
3. Ibid
4. Ibid
5. https://en.wikipedia.org/wiki/Anti-Apartheid_Movement, accessed 28th November 2024
6. Throughline, NPR, The Mandela Effect (podcast), 16th May 2024
7. Oral history interview with Ziggy Melamed as part of Setting the Record Straight project, archived at The Museum of Youth Culture
8. Emma Goldman never said these words, although she did express a similar idea in her 1931 autobiography Living My Life.
9. https://www.theguardian.com/society/2006/dec/13/guardiansocietysupplement3, accessed 5th December 2024
10. Oral history interview with Sheila Freeman as part of Setting the Record Straight project, archived at The Museum of Youth Culture
11. Ibid
12. https://www.theguardian.com/environment/2024/nov/26/how-the-battle-of-claremont-road-changed-the-world-the-whole-of-alternative-london-turned-up, accessed 5th December 2024
13. Oral history interview with Sheila Freeman as part of Setting the Record Straight project, archived at The Museum of Youth Culture
14. https://en.wikipedia.org/wiki/Reclaim_the_Streets, accessed 29th November 2024
15. Oral history interview with Ziggy Melamed as part of Setting the Record Straight project, archived at The Museum of Youth Culture
16. https://en.wikipedia.org/wiki/Reclaim_the_Streets, accessed 29th November 2024
17. Oral history interview with Ziggy Melamed as part of Setting the Record Straight project, archived at The Museum of Youth Culture
18. http://news.bbc.co.uk/onthisday/hi/dates/stories/june/18/newsid_2515000/2515679.stm, accessed 5th December 2024
19. https://en.wikipedia.org/wiki/Carnival_Against_Capital#cite_note-John-13, accessed 5th December 2024
20. Oral history interview with Ziggy Melamed as part of Setting the Record Straight project, archived at The Museum of Youth Culture
21. https://www.spycops.co.uk/the-story/, accessed 5th December 2024
22. https://www.theguardian.com/uk/2013/jun/24/undercover-police-spy-girlfriend-child, accessed 5th December 2024
23. https://www.spycops.co.uk/the-story/, accessed 5th December 2024
24. Oral history interview with Ziggy Melamed as part of Setting the Record Straight project, archived at The Museum of Youth Culture
25. https://www.metamute.org/editorial/articles/reclaiming-asturian-countryside, accessed 27th February 2025
26. Ibid
27. Additional oral history interview with Ziggy Melamed, conducted 23rd January 2025 by Esther Freeman
28. Ibid

29. The Labour Party later went back on this promise, but as Tony Benn says, there is no final victory
30. https://en.wikipedia.org/wiki/Occupy_movement, accessed 5th December 2024
31. https://www.oxfam.org/en/press-releases/ten-richest-men-double-their-fortunes-pandemic-while-incomes-99-percent-humanity, accessed 5th December 2024
32. https://www.trussell.org.uk/news-and-research/latest-stats/end-of-year-stats, accessed 26th March 2025
33. https://www.carersuk.org/reports/state-of-caring-survey-2023-the-impact-of-caring-on-health, accessed 25th March 2025
34. https://www.england.nhs.uk/2023/11/one-in-five-children-and-young-people-had-a-probable-mental-disorder-in-2023/ accessed 25th March 2025
35. Ash Sakar, *Minority Rule, Adventures in the culture war* (2025), p5

Chapter 15: Faiza Rise Up!
1. Faiza Shaheen, *Know Your Place: How Society Sets Us Up to Fail and What We Can Do About It* (2023), Audiobook, Prologue, 0.50
2. https://www.theguardian.com/politics/2013/dec/21/iain-duncan-smith-food-banks-charities, accessed 12th December 2024
3. https://www.thetimes.com/article/welfare-office-made-up-quotes-from-happy-benefits-claimants-pjq38j57x32, accessed 12 December 2024
4. https://www.mirror.co.uk/news/uk-news/murderer-iain-duncan-smith-confronted-7159079 accessed 12 December 2024
5. https://www.theguardian.com/society/2016/may/13/suicides-of-benefit-claimants-reveal-dwp-flaws-says-inquiry, accessed 12 December 2024
6. https://www.theguardian.com/politics/2016/mar/18/iain-duncan-smith-resignation-letter-in-full, accessed 12th December 2024
7. https://members.parliament.uk/constituency/3410/election-history, accessed 12th December 2024
8. Faiza Shaheen, Know Your Place: How Society Sets Us Up to Fail and What We Can Do About It (2023), Audiobook, Prologue, 1.51
9. Ibid, Chapter 3, 01.34
10. Ibid, Chapter 1, 00.48
11. Ibid, Chapter 1 02.58
12. Ibid, Chapter 1, 00.27
13. Ibid, Chapter 6, 00.51
14. Ibid, Chapter 6, 00.57
15. Ibid, Chapter 1 03.18
16. Ibid, Prologue 03.51
17. Ibid, Chapter 10 00.29
18. Ibid, Prologue 04.47
19. Ibid, Prologue 06.50
20. https://www.youtube.com/watch?v=iAIqzYoj1Jc, accessed 12th December 2024
21. https://www.channel4.com/news/exclusive-channel-4-news-obtains-audio-of-faiza-shaheens-labour-candidacy-interview, accessed 12th December 2024
22. https://www.aljazeera.com/news/2024/5/30/appalling-cull-britains-labour-bars-another-leftwinger-from-election, accessed 12th December 2024
23. https://www.independent.co.uk/tv/news/starmer-labour-faiza-shaheen-diane-abbott-b2553961.html, accessed 12th December 2024

24. https://www.theguardian.com/commentisfree/article/2024/may/31/faiza-shaheen-labour-deselected-chingford-woodford-green-general-election, accessed 12th December 2024
25. https://www.middleeasteye.net/news/ex-labour-candidate-excluded-over-pro-palestine-posts-stand-independent, accessed 12th December 2024
26. Ibid
27. https://youtu.be/7i7ajy43GbQ?si=TluTAPUfUpVktof-, accessed 12th December 2024
28. https://www.standard.co.uk/news/politics/iain-duncan-smith-general-election-result-labour-chingford-b1168748.html, accessed 12th December 2024
29. https://www.faizashaheen.co.uk/, accessed 12th December 2024

Conclusion
1. https://www.theatlantic.com/family/archive/2024/11/gen-z-woke-myth-election/680653/, accessed 27th February 2025
2. https://news.sky.com/story/something-remarkable-is-happening-with-gen-z-is-reform-uk-winning-the-bro-vote-13265490, accessed 27th February 2025
3. Ash Sakar, *Minority Rule: Adventures in the culture wars* (2025) p266